The Collaborative Co-Parent

The
Collaborative
Co-Parent

Co-Parenting
MADE DIGNIFIED,
SIMPLE, AND
COLLABORATIVE

GABRIELLA POMARE

NEW YORK

LONDON • NASHVILLE • MELBOURNE • VANCOUVER

The Collaborative Co-Parent

Co-Parenting MADE DIGNIFIED, SIMPLE, AND COLLABORATIVE

Published in New York, New York, by Morgan James Publishing. Morgan James is a trademark of Morgan James, LLC. www.MorganJamesPublishing.com

Proudly distributed by Publishers Group West®

Morgan James BOGO™

A **FREE** ebook edition is available for you or a friend with the purchase of this print book.

CLEARLY SIGN YOUR NAME ABOVE

Instructions to claim your free ebook edition:
1. Visit MorganJamesBOGO.com
2. Sign your name CLEARLY in the space above
3. Complete the form and submit a photo of this entire page
4. You or your friend can download the ebook to your preferred device

ISBN 9781636987033 paperback
ISBN 9781636987040 ebook
Library of Congress Control Number:
2025933849

Cover Design by:
Ale Urquide

Interior Design by:
Chris Treccani
www.3dogcreative.net

Morgan James PUBLISHING **Builds** with... **Habitat for Humanity®** Peninsula and Greater Williamsburg

Morgan James is a proud partner of Habitat for Humanity Peninsula and Greater Williamsburg. Partners in building since 2006.

Get involved today! Visit: www.morgan-james-publishing.com/giving-back

DEDICATION

For my vibrant, cheeky, life-changing, Theodore.
Everything I do is for you.

To my newest joy, Vienna.
You have given me hope, happiness
and an immense love.

And to all co-parents embarking on this journey.
Let's do it with dignity, confidence and . . . collaboratively.

TABLE OF CONTENTS

ACKNOWLEDGMENTS

Writing *The Collaborative Co-Parent* has definitely been, in many ways, a journey. A journey toward a healthier co-parenting relationship for myself in reflecting on the good and bad of what I, and many of my clients and friends, have experienced. It has also been a journey in accomplishing something I so badly wanted to do: share my knowledge and experiences with those who need it most.

I must extend my gratitude to my partner and to my family who supported me through this journey and continually encouraged me to stay motivated and share my story. I am also so thankful to my clients and the people who shared their experiences with me. They taught me just as much as I have guided them. Working with so many strong, resilient people has allowed me to gather information and provide my readers with everyday examples of what works and doesn't work in navigating the co-parenting world. It is only through my own lived experience, and the challenges of those I have worked with and helped, that I have gained perspective in sharing that which I have in this book.

It is important for me to note that while the examples in my book are based on real life experiences, names, ages, and often critical details of my clients' lives have been changed to protect their privacy. Having said that, the emotions, difficulties, and lessons learned by these resilient people are true examples of how this book can be applied and allows readers to gain insight into the differences amongst co-parenting families.

I am grateful to my editor, Sarah Rexford, for taking the time to make this book what it is, and provide me with such valuable guidance and support.

Lastly, thank you, the reader, for trusting in me and being open to embark on the co-parenting journey. Your children will be forever grateful to you for allowing them to experience a more stable, secure, and rewarding future.

INTRODUCTION

So, you separated and you are at the beginning of navigating the co-parenting world. By working together as collaborative co-parents, you protect your children from conflict and the impact of divorce and separation. This book provides a mindful separation and parenting tool. Together, we will navigate this journey and grow strong and resilient children. Separation is not the end—it is the beginning of a new journey providing you with the foundation to create a new type of family with your own rules.

The Collaborative Co-Parent is a modern and timely resource for separated parents. It provides a practical outlook in high conflict, fractured relationships where children are too often caught up in the grief and unhealthy dynamic of a separating family. Our philosophy is simple: co-parenting made dignified, simple, and collaborative.

When picking up this book, you probably thought, "But what is a collaborative co-parent?" Let me start with this. If you lie in bed awake at night following a marriage breakdown or end of a relationship think about the following, this book is for you:

- What happens now?
- How do we both raise the kids?
- This feels complicated.

- The road ahead seems daunting.

You are on your way to becoming a more collaborative co-parent. No one said it would be easy or that this book would have all the answers. We know that separation brings trauma, all sorts of stressors, and never-ending challenges. These make it difficult to look forward and into the future. We also know, and social science and research tell us, that children do best in environments where there is stability. It is your role as a parent to encourage that stability. A collaborative co-parent is someone who recognizes the challenges ahead but wants to prioritize their child's need for stability, love, security, as well as their right to have a safe relationship with both parents.

A collaborative co-parent recognizes that separation is the time to put your children's wellbeing ahead of your own and to make decisions that allow your children to be raised in the healthiest and happiest way possible. I know that it is not always easy to make these decisions on your own, particularly without practical assistance such as a roadmap for how to navigate your future. That's where I come in.

It is important to remember that although your relationship is over, you are still a family. Acknowledging this and putting your children's needs ahead of anger and conflict will allow you to co-parent in a more effective way. *The Collaborative Co-Parent* provides you with the cornerstone to restructure your family dynamic so that with the right rules and tools in place, as separated parents you can coexist (and hopefully even get on!). Let's jump on board the journey. Together, we've got this . . .

CHAPTER 1:

So, You've Separated. Now what?

Transitioning from Spouse to Co-Parent

Silence. You're awake and your eyes scour the room. You can hear every little sound the house makes. Your bed feels empty and that sinking feeling in your belly grows stronger. You feel alone. Even a little lost. Is it really over? Now what?

This is likely the first time in a long time that you have been on your own. It is probably the first time in a long time that you have the power to make your own decisions and to navigate how your life will look from here on out.

Let me start out by saying you have got this and I am so proud of you. Just by picking this book up from the shelf, you have made the choice to be informed about the co-parenting journey. By reading this book you are making an active decision to better your co-parenting relationship. By working together as collaborative co-parents, you are protecting your children from conflict and the impact of divorce and separation. Together, we will navigate this journey and encourage our children to become strong and resilient.

Let's be honest. Divorce, separation, or the end of a relationship sucks. Whether you wanted this change or not, there is little doubt that you are experiencing a rollercoaster of emotions. There will be days when you don't want to get out of bed. Days when the thought of making school lunches and getting your child off to school seems impossible. And there will be many days where you don't turn up to friends' parties, family functions, or lunch dates. You just want to curl up in bed, reflect, and even cry. Feeling like this is completely fine. In fact, it's normal.

If you didn't want to cry every time a rom com played on TV, or walked past a young couple holding hands, I'd almost say there *must* be something wrong with you.

There will, however, be days when you feel awesome. When you wake up wanting to try a new juice cleanse, jump on the treadmill, or go out for a long lunch with friends. You will feel the "new me" mentality and try one hundred different things until you feel refreshed and revived. You will paint your living room a new color, buy some new furniture, and maybe even try a whole new hairstyle.

"Divorce isn't such a tragedy. A tragedy's staying in an unhappy marriage, teaching your children the wrong things about love. Nobody ever died of divorce."

—Jennifer Weiner

The healing process is a slow one. Despite what they tell you, nobody heals from a separation overnight. It takes time, mistakes, and new experiences. Eventually things will start to feel a little normal again.

The Healing Process

I can tell you from personal experience that when I separated, I woke up every day for at least a month thinking, "Did that actually happen? Is this the new normal? Am I going to be alone forever?"

You're not. Life does move on as quickly as you allow it. You are in control. This is your life. As much as I wanted to stay in bed and book a flight to Europe to find myself, within minutes of my daydreaming, I would be brought back to reality by a little voice yelling out *mamma*. And just like that, I remembered I had another person to think about, someone who was even more important than me. Someone I needed to protect, whose feelings I needed to safeguard, and who I needed to ensure felt loved and secure.

In hindsight, the morning cuddles, the sticky fingers, and the need to quickly reorganize my life to juggle work commitments, preschool drop-offs and pick-ups, and create a sense of normality is probably what helped me the most. Despite feeling like I had failed and that a divorce was the worst thing ever, I had a little person to chase after and who loved me more than anything in the world. That feeling is like no other.

I often talk about separation or divorce as a rollercoaster or a journey. Most of the clients I work with come in my door one person, and twelve to eighteen months later, leave an entirely different person. I can tell you this isn't because of the legal battle they have just been through, but rather because of the way time naturally gifts us periods to grieve, to soul search, to find hope, and to plan our new future. By looking at separation as an opportunity for something new, we will gradually climb out of bed, and literally hop, skip, and jump into the exciting new future that awaits.

By focusing on this, the co-parenting journey becomes easier, too. When we allow ourselves to become stuck in grief, stuck in anger, and unable to move past the hurt or the conflict, we essential force our children to also become stuck in the limbo of negativity. We stop our children from experiencing life. But by promoting a healthier co-parenting relationship, we give both ourselves and our children the opportunity to move forward and experience a sense of hope about the future.

If we can learn to separate the anger and hurt from our role as parents, role models, example setters, we can be better parents (and indeed co-parents). The power is with you to do this. Don't wait for your co-parent to start. Take this opportunity to create a new pathway forward. Pick a direction, jump on board, and get started.

Telling the Children: What's Appropriate and What to Avoid

Although the heartbreak and variety of emotions you are experiencing seem impossible, you need to remember that there are little (or big) people who need to know what is going on. Little brains are trying to work out why their parents aren't living together anymore (or aren't in the same bedroom, if that is the case for you). There are probably little minds scrambling to work out why there has been yelling or tears, and maybe even suitcases or boxes coming and going. If you feel like the rollercoaster of emotions that you are riding is pretty big, try to imagine how big your child's rollercoaster may seem as they attempt to work out what is going on and probably also feel a little to blame.

Too many people I work with come in and tell me, "The kids don't know we are separating." My client, Stefanie (client names have been changed for their privacy), had been with me for about six months. Despite having been separated for almost twelve months, dating, and being involved in high-conflict divorce proceedings, she would go home each night and pretend she and her ex were in an intact marriage.

She would wash her ex's clothes, cook dinner for everyone, and then once the children were in bed, would take herself to sleep on the lounge downstairs. She would make sure she woke up early enough to pack away the blankets and hide any piece of evidence that there was an issue in the home.

At the same time, she would tell me about the dates she had been on, the parties she was going to with other single moms, and the snarky remarks her ex would make in front of the children including: "Mom's forgotten about us. She's going out again," or "I can't afford that new bike. Your mom's trying to take all my money."

The reality was, her children knew what was going on and she was trying to mask the truth. Her teenage children were likely coming up with all sorts of scenarios about what was happening, and probably siding with dad simply because he was being more honest. Her children needed her to have the conversation with them and for her to be open and honest with them about their futures.

How to tell your children their parents are separating can feel like the world's worst conversation. How do you prepare yourself to break little hearts? My view is that it is better for children to live in two separate homes with happy, healthy, and strong parents. The worst thing for a child is living in a home where there is constant conflict, yelling, slamming of doors, or even worse, two parents who do not communicate and live separate lives.

As adults, we often forget that children's brains are always developing. Even the youngest of kids are affected by conflict and arguments. Their normal environment becomes one where negativity and unhealthy adult relationships are a constant.

How you ultimately decide to tell your children about your separation or divorce will very depending on their age and stage of development. If you have kids at different stages in their lives, it can also be useful to tell them in different ways. This will help them to understand and process what is happening a little better.

There may be parents who can sit down as a team to speak with their children. However, there will be other situations where it is impossible to have that discussion as a family. Your dynamic, post separation, may be too high conflict, emotions may be raw, or you may simply feel unable to sit with your partner face-to-face so soon after your breakup.

There is no right or wrong way, and you should not feel like a failure because of the way you break the news to your children. Hang in there. This is life-changing and you are doing your best. The important part is what you tell your children and the way you help them manage their emotions.

Before you sit down to tell your children, it is important that you and your co-parent are on the same page about what message to give. How are you going to tell them and what are you going to say? How will you tackle their big emotions and how will you each reassure your children things are going to be okay? Think about your child's age and maturity level. What language should be used? How can you make sure your child understands and feels supported?

Determining the best forum to tell your children about your divorce or separation will depend on the circumstances. Some great ways my clients have done this include:

- Family dinner night where the children pick what's on the menu.
- Movie and popcorn night to follow a big discussion.
- A family walk/park date.
- Picnic at your child's favorite park where they can have a break to play.
- Pancake and waffle breakfast.

First and foremost, children need to feel supported and loved by both of their parents. The first thing a child needs to know is that irrespective of what is happening, and despite the change, their parents will continue being their parents. They need to know you both will always be there to listen, to encourage, and to love them. Even where it is not possible for you and your ex to sit down together with your children, it is so important that you make clear to your children that you still support their other parent, and that your child will always have two parents who want what is best for them.

Children do not need to be told the ins and outs of what went wrong in your relationship. They definitely do not need to know who might have cheated or who complained too much. This isn't an opportunity to try and win over your child and prove who is the better parent.

However, children do need to know the practical reality of what is happening and the plan for their future. Reassurance is everything. This includes reassurance about things like living arrangements, friends, extended families, and school. The first thing kids often worry about is how often they can see their cousins, whether they need to change schools, and what having two bedrooms might feel like. Will they have two of their favorite posters on the wall or fluffy pillow that helps them fall asleep? Although these things might seem trivial to parents, they are huge issues for children. By addressing these issues, you provide your child safety and security.

My friend, Lara, decided to tell her three-year-old and six-year-old boys about her divorce from her husband Steve, about four months after they made the decision. She waited until the big lifestyle choices had been decided: what properties would be sold, who would live where, and what school the boys would attend. In this case, because her children were so young, it helped them to have the big decisions already put in place as they transitioned from a one-unit family to children with co-parents.

There are obviously some exceptions to honesty being the best policy. I am a big believer in being open and honest with your children about their new reality, but where you have younger children, big decisions often have to be made and some things kept from your children until the time is right. There is no one size fits all approach to this. We are all learning and making mistakes and learning again. It is important to step back and assess your situation to make a decision about what should be said and when.

Her divorce was a little high conflict because of an affair. To make sure neither party became agitated or said things out of line during the conversation with her boys, Lara organized a dinner with the boys and their aunt and uncle, with whom they had a close bond. All four adults sat down over a meal with the boys. They had an open chat about mom and dad moving into two separate apartments and how exciting this would be for the boys. They would get to pick new furniture, toys, and books for their new bedrooms. Both parents reassured the boys that they would continue to be loved by each parent, their extended family members, and friends.

Lara told me it was incredibly helpful to have her sister and brother-in-law present to help keep things calm and the children focused and positive. It also worked well to reassure the boys that their family would continue to be around and support them. For the next few weeks, before bed time, she picked some relevant bedtime stories about separation and moving homes, to help ease the idea of change with her boys.

Knowing what is planned for their future will have a huge impact on how your children navigate the separation process and cope with the changes in their lives. Doing things like going out and buying new bedding, allowing kids to decorate their own bedrooms, organizing play dates with friends, and encouraging open discussion help make the separation process easier for children. If there are going to be big changes like school or homes, encourage children to be involved in the process (depending on their maturity levels) and let them feel they have some control of the changes. The more in control they feel, the easier the transition will seem.

"There are things in my life that are hard to reconcile, like divorce. Sometimes it is very difficult to make sense of how it could possibly happen. Laying blame is so easy. I don't have time for hate or negativity in my life. There's no room for it."

—Reece Witherspoon

One change at a time is often best. Changing homes, schools, friends, and communities all at once is overwhelming. Where possible, break things down. Stay in the home as long as you can. Go to school open days together. Enroll your kids in local activities like football or ballet where they might make friends who go to the new school. Little things like this can make a big difference.

Above all else, be clear that your separation or divorce is not your child's fault. Children will naturally feel guilt and question whether they caused the separation. It is our job as parents to reassure children that the breakdown of the relationship was not caused by them at all. It should be made clear that the best way to be a good parent is for parents to be happy. And in some circumstances, parents need to be apart to be happy and be better parents. This is never anyone's fault, but decisions are made by adults to ensure their children can lead happy lives. Blame should never be raised. Playing the blame game will never benefit the child.

Lastly, as difficult as having this conversation is, it is so important to keep your emotions in check. Do not plan to discuss your separation with your children until you are able to refrain from displaying anger, hurt, or upset. Whilst it's perfectly normal to have these feelings, it is detrimental to a child's security and development to see these emotions in this context. Children naturally feel guilty and are largely impacted by the way information is communicated and by what they see. By displaying positivity and showing respect to your co-parent, you set a healthy pathway for your children to cope with how separation will change their family. You also reduce a child's fears and anxieties about change and remove the need for a child to feel like they need to pick sides.

My advice? Planning is everything. Think things through. Try to have answers to the questions your child is likely to ask and remember, it won't be easy. It is often helpful to work with a good family therapist or child counselor/psychologist to assist in understanding the best way to both start this type of conversation and navigate your child's emotions.

The First Stages of Uncoupling

Divorce and separation are transient processes. How you feel and the decisions you make one month after a breakup will be inherently different twelve months and even a few years later. Indeed, how you interact with your co-parent will evolve and develop as time goes on. Some co-parents find it impossible to get on after separation, but a few years down the track, they realize how important the co-parent relationship is for their child and develop a strong co-parenting bond.

We often see a significant difference in the way each parent copes and deals with the breakup. If you are the person who wants to move on, change will be appealing and you may make a more active effort to co-parent sooner than your previous partner. However, if you are the parent who wants to stay and work things out, you will likely experience a range of emotions. This emotion will affect the way you handle change and adapt to seeing your ex as a co-parent rather than a partner.

"It's sad, something coming to an end. It cracks you open, in a way—cracks you open to feeling. When you try to avoid the pain, it creates greater pain."

—Jennifer Aniston

So, how do you go from partners to co-parents? How does the person you wanted to spend your life with, in a romantic sense, become more of a business-like partner with whom you share a common purpose? Can the brain really re-wire itself and learn to view such a significant person differently? With time, yes.

You would be surprised how many clients I work with who at the time of separation, cannot see past the hurt and upset. They cannot even contemplate a world where they would co-parent their children with their ex. Their lives are filled with nasty text message exchanges, closed conversations, lies, deceit, and anger.

Fast forward a few years to when I check in to see how things have progressed. The majority of these people have found a way to work together and co-parent successfully. It is often the case that emotions are still too raw after separation to clearly see what is best for your child. That is no criticism for you or for anyone. It's the reality of going through a big trauma and life change.

The positive takeaway is that once the dust settles and you find your way, there will come a time when making joint decisions about your child will be easier. Sending a message to update your ex about your child's progress during the week or sharing a few photos from a holiday won't seem like the impossible.

I will never forget my client, Kane, who went through a four-year litigation battle in the Family Court. His wife was trying everything to stop him from having anything but supervised time with their son. She even made an application to relocate overseas with their son. There seemed to be no way these two adults would see past their differences to co-parent their child. I remember emailing him a few years later to check in. He emailed back immediately with photos of him and his son overseas in Disneyland.

He had managed to work hard with his ex in family therapy to develop a good enough parenting relationship where they could now work collaboratively, and he was spending time overseas on holidays with his son. I could not wipe the smile off my face. I don't know whether it was disbelief or pure happiness, but either way, what a gift for their young boy!

Emotions play a big part in the uncoupling process. Whether it is how you feel about your former partner or how you feel about the process of divorce or separation, these thoughts and feelings generally shape how you go about transitioning from lovers to co-parents. There is nothing wrong with having feelings. It is our emotions that make us human and help us to cope. It is experiencing those emotions that bring us to understanding and clarity. Indeed, if we ignored our emotions and try to hide them away, they generally multiply and eventually take over in a negative, unmanageable way.

In my experience, I found that where I tried to ignore feelings of sadness or anger, and admittedly some days, hate, those feelings found themselves in my text messages, emails, and sometimes even in hostile face to face communications in the early days. This ultimately made things worse for my co-parenting relationship.

My inability to address my emotions and allow myself to feel created a toxic communication style. This caused havoc on my ability to nurture a positive and healthy co-parenting style for my son. It was only when I looked my feelings in the face and allowed myself to work through those emotions that I understood why I was feeling the way I was. I had to process the anger and the confusion to focus on what was important in life and how to best parent my son.

Whether it is by journaling, working with a professional such as a therapist, or even exercising, the processing of emotion is key to moving forward. You will also find that by allowing yourself to experience the emotion that comes with separation, you encourage the healing process. This will, in turn, benefit your children.

My girlfriend, Lara, told me it took her months before she was able to really shift her focus and view her ex-husband in a different light. Still, when she saw her daughter do something cute, the first person she wanted to text was her ex. When she saw something nice at the shops, her inclination was to send a quick snap to her ex. She thought about him most mornings and nights, and no matter what activity she was doing, she often felt sadness about not doing it with him.

By cutting communication for a few months and limiting exchanges to a more businesslike approach to parenting, she was able to re-shift her focus, gain momentum in terms of her solo life, and slowly rewired her brain into seeing her ex as more of a parenting partner. Her communications with him slowly became only about school events, routine, the wellbeing of her children, and drop-off locations.

Stefanie told me of her inability to initially stop obsessing about her ex's new life. She spent hours scrolling social media to see what he was doing, who he was socializing with, and where he was going. She would try to piece all the online snippets together to create a fantasy in her mind of what his new life looked like. This would extend to who he was sleeping with, where he was holidaying, what he was doing with their children.

It was only by completely shutting off from social media and ceasing any communication about their personal lives that she could let go of the unhealthy obsession and focus on her life and her co-parenting relationship. At the end of the day, what he did was irrelevant. All that mattered was that her children were safe, loved, and taken care of, and that Stefanie and her ex had a mutual understanding about how to continue parenting their children.

Early Days Navigating the Separated Family Unit

Boundaries are a big part of transitioning from romantic partners to co-parents. It can be so difficult to process the change in the relationship. To navigate the change, you need to be able to put into place rules and strategies for how you communicate (which we explore in the next chapter), as well as the information you exchange. As much as you might want to know about your ex-partner's new life, sometimes less information is better.

You aren't in a romantic relationship anymore. Your relationship really is limited to making decisions about your child and determining what is best for your child on the long road ahead. This doesn't mean you can't sit down for a coffee or have a chat at drop-off, but you need to be clear in your head where your relationship sits and what your common purpose is.

The way to encourage a healthy transition is often to limit the interactions between you and your co-parent and restrict communication to focus only on your child. In the first few months, this might be limited to discussing changes to parenting arrangements and routine, daycare or school issues, and dealing with preliminary teething issues. Is one of your children bedwetting out of the blue? Or are your children playing you off against each other? Will one eat vegetables with you but not with their other parent? It can be helpful to discuss these types of issues with your co-parent to foster open dialogue and keep you focused on the common purpose.

However, during the early days of separation, if you shift communication to more friendly, personal dialogues (such as which restaurant you visited last weekend, how great your new home is, or the holiday you have coming up), this can stir emotions and often slow your transition to healthy co-parents. Limit any discussion that you know will bring up bad memories or cause you to overthink, feel guilt, feel blame, or even jealousy. These are unhealthy emotions which, whilst normal to have, can negatively impact the goal you are aiming for.

Also consider whether you and your co-parent will benefit from maintaining an online relationship, such as being friends on social media. Things like photos, comments, or interactive stories can often be misconstrued and cause one to jump to conclusions that end in conflict. It is not always healthy to see pictures of your children at the beach with your co-parent and other friends or new partners when you are still dealing with the emotions that come with relationship breakdown.

Perhaps limit what you share on social media or consider taking time away from being connected online. There may come a time where you can have a healthy and positive online relationship, but if you feel like seeing your co-parent's posts might trigger a negative reaction or cause you to feel sadness or hurt, you are better off removing each other as online friends as you uncouple. I have found that people often jump to conclusions when they see photos or online posts out of context, which in turn encourages arguments for no real reason. A photo isn't always what you think and what people portray online is rarely what is happening in reality. Sometimes it is better not to know.

Remember, there will be good and bad times. All transitions bring highs and lows. There is no such thing as the perfect divorce, but there are imperfect relationships and less than perfect people. No one expects you to behave perfectly after a relationship breakdown, and playing the blame game is hard to avoid. Separation often brings with it attempts to reconcile, arguments about what's best for the kids, and sometimes even legal proceedings.

Friends will side with one of you and extended families experience the separation, too. You will lose friends and even family members, but you will find new ones and in time. You will heal. It is all about perspective and focus. How you navigate co-parenting communication, cope with struggles with defiant children, engage with new partners or blended families, and handle breakdowns in your co-parenting relationship largely depend on the knowledge and guidance you obtain.

The important thing in all of this is that you remember that there is no such thing as a broken family. Just because your marriage didn't last doesn't mean your children have to experience drastic change. You did not fail. You have been given an opportunity to work as co-parents and create a nurturing, safe, and secure family unit for your children, albeit in two homes. There are so many exciting aspects of co-parenting, and even advantages to your children.

When tension and conflict are removed from the home environment, children often feel more relaxed. When learning to adapt to having two homes and the differences that come with separated parents, children become more resilient and adaptable to change. These are significant life lessons that children will carry into their adult lives.

CHAPTER 2

Communication Is Everything

*Tools and Resources to Encourage Healthy,
Safe Communication with Your Ex*

Picking up the phone and hearing your ex-partner's voice after a difficult breakup is tough. It will often rile up a range of emotions you have tried hard to suppress in order to move on. When there has been toxicity in your relationship and home environment, communication can almost seem impossible.

I remember that during the first few weeks of separating, I felt almost confused as to what was too much communication and what was not enough. Did I have to tell my child's father everything that was going on day to day? Did we need to speak daily? I still wanted to share photos and videos of memories and experiences, but was that too much?

There is little doubt that every relationship is different. The dynamics among each set of co-parents will differ from couple to couple. Navigating what type of communication works best and how much of it is appropriate will take time (and will often change as life changes and children grow). There will be stages in your child's life where it feels like you and your ex are constantly talking, and there will be other times when there will be little need to communicate outside of business-like emails and updates.

I am certainly not here to preach that my way is the right one, but I can tell you that for me, there is one absolutely fundamental aspect to healthy co-parenting, and that is communication. To me, communication is absolutely everything.

There is little doubt that the end of a relationship is an incredibly distressing and emotional time. You will go through a whirlwind of feelings, from sadness, to anger, to guilt, to regret, and even a desire to go back to the way things were. The biggest challenge is how to move forward and give yourself space when you have children and must see or hear from your ex-spouse or ex-lover. How do you shift your mindset from couple to co-parents, and how do you work out the ins and outs of communicating effectively together, despite the anger or hurt?

"Co-parenting. It's not a competition between two homes. It's a collaboration of parents doing what is best for the kids."

—**Heather Hetchler**

By implementing tools to set boundaries around your communication, what seems difficult at the start can become second nature in no time. Take it from me—this doesn't happen overnight. Communicating with an ex is tough and can seem impossible in the first few days, weeks, months, and even years. But you will get there, and it will become easier. Trust me, your kids will thank you for protecting them from the conflict and exemplifying what healthy communication looks like.

You can model for them how to communicate with others as they grow and develop. Your communication style can set a roadmap for your children to avoid arguments, speak with respect, listen with understanding, and reflect on their responses.

So where to from here? The first part, I suppose, comes down to identifying what method of communication works best. This will undoubtedly differ from family to family depending on circumstances, level of conflict, risk issues, and the topic that needs discussing. It is important in the early days to set boundaries around what issue requires what type of communication.

If it's urgent (think a health crisis such as a trip to the emergency room) a phone call is always best. If it's to discuss a change to parenting arrangements, routine, or your child's development, an email might be best. If it's to do with day-to-day issues including ballet shoes left at the other's house or an upcoming school play, a text message can likely do the trick. There are, in my opinion, four essential pillars to healthy co-parenting communication.

Listening

The first thing to remember when it comes to the first pillar of effective communication is to respect where each of you sit in terms of the separation. If you were the person who ended the relationship, it is likely you have had a little more time to process and come to terms with your new reality.

Pause to remember that your ex-partner is likely still in the grieving stage. This really needs to be considered when starting to communicate again. You are both on this new journey from parenting together as a couple, to co-parenting between two homes. The dynamic has changed, and most likely, your communication style has changed.

When starting a conversation with your co-parent, it is so important to make sure that you do not boast about your new life or put down their lifestyle choices or changes. Let the other parent know they have not been left behind. Rather, you are both navigating this new separated life with the common goal of ensuring your child feels safe, secure, loved, and respected.

This is where the need to listen comes in. Whether it's a face-to-face conversation, an email, a text message, or a phone call, let the other person speak . . . and finish. Don't jump in, don't speak over each other, and remember you are speaking with your child's other parent, not an enemy. Your relationship with this person is not going to end tomorrow. You need to find a way to make it work for the sake of your child.

Listening, however, doesn't mean simply keeping silent and letting the other person finish. For communication to be effective, you need to actively hear and understand what your co-parent is saying. This means actively following the conversation, digesting the message being said, engaging in terms of a nod or smile, and properly taking in the words being used so that you can pause and reflect.

Your role as a listener is ultimately to take in the message and properly understand. What I often find beneficial is to paraphrase the other person to ensure the right message is coming across. For example, "It sounds like you are saying . . ." or "Am I right to understand . . ."

> *"You can't go wrong by showing interest in what other people say and making them feel important. In other words, the better you listen, the more you'll be listened to."*
>
> **—Jarvis, T.**

This helps to ensure the message is not being misunderstood, which often encourages an unhelpful or inflammatory response.

Just as listening means paying attention and showing respect to the person who is speaking, it also means ignoring emotionally inflammatory language (whether in person, by email, or in text). The best part of actually listening is that you get to pick and choose the information that you store in your brain for later.

We know that storing aggressive or emotional conversations does nothing for our mental health and wellbeing. The best thing to do in these situations is to ignore, nod, and move on (or leave the conversation, if required).

Similarly, as a parent, it is imperative that while you to listen to your co-parent, you keep your children from any child-related or adult type communication. It is your first and foremost role to protect your child from witnessing, overhearing, listening, and participating in any communication which may negatively impact their relationship with their other parent.

If your co-parent tries to start communication during a changeover, end the conversation and let them know you will reconvene at a later time, without your child present. Password protect your emails and text messages and don't share these with your child—even when emotional.

The Need to Pause

Pause. Don't shoot from the hip. Take a deep breath. Digest. Easier said than done, right? There is a reason I am telling you to pause before responding. Experience tells us that when you are communicating with someone you probably would rather not ever speak to again, you are already on guard. You will feel emotional to the point where even positive things may sound hurtful or aggressive.

Just speaking with your co-parent might catch you off guard. The best thing you can do in this situation, and any time you are in communication with your co-parent is to pause. Imagine how much better your responses and the flow of your conversation may be if you take a little bit of time to process.

It is not for me to tell you to take three seconds, three minutes, three hours, or even three days to respond (the nature of the communication will often tell you that). For example, if you receive an email that asks you to consider a change to your parenting routine or schedule, or proposes an overseas trip with your child, you might want to take a few days to process before responding.

If you wake up to an SMS from your co-parent accusing you of forgetting to put sunscreen on your child during your visit to the beach over the weekend, you might want to take a few hours before angrily typing back a response. If you talking face-to-face or chatting via phone and are taken by surprise by a request they make or some new information and don't have three days to respond, take a breath. Take a few seconds, explain you need a minute, and take time for yourself. Everyone deserves a minute. Your brain (and probably your heart) will thank you for it in the long run!

People often say that when you feel frustrated or triggered, it is best to be silent. This is another reason why the pause is so important. This is particularly relevant during the early days or weeks following a separation, when emotions are flying high, you are unsure of your future, and when communications with an ex-partner can seem impossible. Emotion takes over. You want to yell, scream, tell them all the things they did wrong, all the hurt they have caused.

At the same time though, you need to organize school drop-offs and pick-ups, enrollment in extra-curricular activities, change-overs, medications, sleep routines, and work out the way forward. By implementing these tools, you can have these much-needed conversations without angst or anxiety. The best part of communication post-separation is that you have the control. You can decide how long you need before coming back with an answer.

Too often, we send an email without thinking, we fight back by text message, or we let our anger get the better of us in a difficult face-to-face conversation. We all know better, but these automatic reactions continue happening. It is not until we consciously listen and become aware of our need for a pause that we will actually stop ourselves from reacting and instead, move on to reflect.

"Effective parenting has nothing to do with pointing out our faults and everything to do with working out solutions."

—L. R. Knost

The power of a pause gives us the time and space to see an issue clearly, take control of the situation, and decide how we respond. The power of that decision is everything. Without a pause, we instinctively react without any real thought or consideration of the most appropriate way forward . . . and often experience regret. The power of the pause allows us to be aware, to be objective, and to have real perspective.

Why Reflection Is So Important During Any Type of Communication

The beauty of the pause is that it gives us time to breathe, contemplate, and reflect on what we have been told. With time to reflect, we are able to compose ourselves, manage emotions, and feel emotionally safe during our communications.

The benefit of reflection is the ability to place boundaries around the manner of communication and to regain control over the tone of the conversation. You may have been thrown a series of demands or questions concerning forthcoming school holiday time or your new relationship and how and when that person interacts with your child.

When you pause, you get to choose how you respond and how you steer the next wave of communication. By reflecting, you take back the power to understand, obtain perspective, think more flexibly, and minimize possible conflict.

During your period of reflection, weigh the pros and cons of the topic. It is always important to be open minded and see the issue from several perspectives. It can often be helpful to toss around ideas with your nearest and dearest. They can offer a third-party view and hopefully sensible and productive advice.

When you are too close to the core of an issue, emotion often takes over. A close friend or family member might be able to see reason a little easier and help you sensibly look for alternative options.

It can often also help to put yourself in your child's shoes. What really is in their best interest? Reflection means considering not what will make you happiest but what will be the best possible outcome for your child.

Reflection can be harder depending on the type of communication. There is little doubt that when faced with an in-person discussion or a surprise phone call, you often feel the need to immediately respond without any real consideration of what has been put to you.

It is a great idea to work with your co-parent on a roadmap for communication that will work for you. This roadmap often depends on the context or issue, but with appropriate communication protocols, you can create time to pause and reflect before responding. In my experience, co-parents manage

"Make a positive difference in your children's lives. Act and speak about your co-parent with respect and integrity."
—Allison Pescosolido

communication best when they have talked through conversation rules and acceptable modes of communication.

Where possible, try to implement the following modes of communication that will allow you to have more time to think and really consider your responses.

- **Planned meetings:** With a meeting is planned, you can set an agenda and take time to reflect on the important issues to discuss. These might happen biannually, when you need to chat about more important issues such as international travel, school, or behavioral issues. A public setting is often useful to avoid rising tempers and risk of conflict.
- **Email:** Email works well when you want to put a more difficult proposal to your co-parent. Remember to use polite, respectful, and business-like language. Use a descriptive subject line and break your email up into discussion points. This often helps to achieve a more productive reply and keeps the conversation flowing. Email is also great because you can open, read, pause, and reflect on your own terms and in your own time.
- **Text message:** Messages are helpful for urgent issues or times when you need a quick response. Again, try to keep your language conflict free. A text is not a way to shame another parent, criticize, or blame. Instead, it is a productive way to inform your co-parent if you are running late to changeover, to enquire about lost school shoes, or to ask for help with school drop-off last minute. When you are the recipient of a text message, have the respect to read and determine the urgency for a response. There is nothing worse than ignoring a message that required a rather timely response. If you have read it, and it is straightforward and

does not require long reflection, respond as soon as possible and be done with the issue. Conflict free texting is key.

- **Parenting apps:** In this modern age, co-parents are blessed to have several phone apps available to download. These provide a safe space for parents to communicate. This is particularly important for parents whose relationship ended on bad terms, is high conflict, or where there is a history of violence. Apps can show you when messages are sent/received and whether they have been read. Exchanging messages in a neutral and secure environment often reduces the risk of conflict. This also allows parents to feel safer, open up, and communicate effectively. Through your co-parenting app you can share photos, events, newsletters, and the like. You can also take time to receive information, reflect on it, and consider the best way forward before reengaging with the app.

Responding (Often the Toughest Part)

As difficult as it may seem at first, the key to healthy co-parent communication is that it is civil, courteous, and respectful. Remember, you model what a positive relationship looks like to your child.

What often works best (when engaging in email, text message, or on an app) is to draft a response and sit on it. I suppose you could say that this is a blend of reflect and respond. This is particularly important if you have received an inflammatory communication and automatically draft a response during a state of heightened emotion.

I often suggest sending the text to a friend or saving your email to drafts. Take some time to reflect, then come back. You will likely re-draft your response to something emotionally neutral and effective. We all experience the desire to fight fire with fire, but responding in a civil and respectful manner will always achieve your desired outcome more effectively.

If the initial communication is inflammatory, you are probably best to ignore it. Instead, craft a response which is to the point, informative, and sticks to the issue at hand. There is no place for emotion in business-like communication (which is often what works best following separation). Think about it. Would you send your boss or colleague a highly emotional text or email when in a state of anger? Probably not. Your child won't benefit from this type of communication between their parents, either.

Some tips: Use plain language, be as pleasant as you can, avoid CAPS, keep your communication informative and to the point, and avoid intrusive questions.

How you structure your communication will often depend on the message you intend to deliver. Do you need to pass on information? Are you looking to resolve an issue that has been on the back burner about your child's schooling or wellbeing? Or are you merely communicating to make a point or start an argument?

If it is the latter, do not send. These types of communication are the ones that should be sent to a friend or stored away in your draft emails as a reminder of unproductive and unhelpful communication.

You will likely find that as the months and years go on, you require less time to pause and reflect. Pleasant, productive communication will become easier and more regular. Communication about big issues will seem less arduous once you both master the four pillars to effective communication.

Experience tells us that the best responses steer clear of a need to defend or justify your position. Do you want to take your child on a holiday during the other parent's time? A simple *"I would like to take Rose to Hawaii during the first week of the school holidays. Can we talk about swapping weeks?"* will encourage a better response than a spiel about how you haven't been on holidays forever, that Rose has been down because of the separation, or that you need some time out from life. The background story often encourages a high conflict and emotionally driven response, which can in turn lead to an argument.

Try to keep your communication child-focused. Usually, the only reason you need to communicate following a separation is because of your child. So, keep that special boy or girl at the forefront of your mind when composing your responses. With a child-focused response, you are more likely to achieve a child-focused outcome.

If a response is required face-to-face during a conversation or over the phone, your body language and tone of voice are more important than anything.

A few tips: Avoid the eye roll, don't laugh or smirk, there is no need for raised voices, and if you can't compose yourself, it is often best to walk away.

So, why improve your communication? Above everything, it is important to remember that it is your most important role as a parent, and indeed more so as a co-parent, to protect your child from hurt, upset, confusion, and feelings of guilt.

When parents are unable to communicate effectively, children are too often dragged into adult conflict, forced to pick sides, send messages, and keep secrets. What parents often don't realize is the significant negative impact this has on their child's future development.

The signs aren't always immediately obvious, but social science tells us that children turn into teenagers who turn into adults that have difficulties forming relationships, communicating, concentrating, and generally coping with life when they have been embroiled in unnecessary conflict during their early years.

Children should not be made to feel like they need to align with either parent. They should not be used as messengers to discuss changeovers or routine. They should not be involved in or placed in hearing distance of any communication that negatively discusses their other parent.

Children of separation need reassurance, love, and stability. They need to see their parents communicating despite no longer being together. Children need to know that although their family unit may have changed, they still belong to a family and their life won't be majorly disrupted.

You have the power to change how you communicate and to give your child the gift of harmony, unity, and security.

Now it's time to consider your communication plan. Use this space to set out a communication plan that will work for you.

We can best communicate using . . .

When a point of conflict arises, we will . . .

> **The boundaries we need to put in place are . . .**
>
>
>
>
>
>
>
>
>

I know that for me, emails tend to work best for changes to schedules, requests for holidays, and the like. Text messages are great for day-to-day updates. We schedule a call if something particularly urgent has arisen or we have concerns that need a proper discussion (for example, when we wanted to change our son's pre-school).

Something that worked well for me recently was a daily update by way of text message when I travelled overseas for a few weeks and my son stayed with his dad. Each day I would get a message updating me about my son's eating habits, sleeping, and general mood/news. This was comforting because I felt like I was not missing out on any changes and it assisted me to keep track of his progress (particularly his sleeping routine!).

Encouraging Communication Between Children and Their Other Parent

Just as the way we model communication between co-parents is essential, so is the way we model encouragement of communication between our co-parent and our child.

I often get asked what works for me. At the same time, I am often criticized for the way I do things when it comes to communication. It took time to work out what would be best for our situation. Things have also evolved over the years as my son grew from a young one-year-old to a cheeky preschooler. I am a big believer in video communication.

When a child can't be with both parents each day, I think there is something special and important about having that face-to-face interaction with the non-resident parent—even if only for a few minutes. That is the key, however. Parents cannot expect or demand their child to stay on the phone or video call for a set amount of time.

I have so many clients who come to me demanding parenting orders requiring their child to stay on the phone for at least thirty minutes at a time. This is unrealistic. Children will be children. If there is ever a time for flexibility, it is in the way you approach your communication style with your child.

When my son was younger, I would try to video call him daily. This took encouragement and effort by his father to set up the call and try to engage him. Some days the calls would last a minute or so, a quick "hello" or an "I love you." I knew that seeing me was important and it showed him that his parents could be civil enough to facilitate some telephone time.

As he has grown, the calls generally happen either during breakfast or after preschool so we can chat about his day. Again, this requires an active effort on both our parts to make time for calls, answer them, and try to keep our son engaged on the call. A simple text to arrange a good time is what works best for us. Texting also helps ensure there is an understanding if other things come up such as unexpected guests or if our son is just having a bad day.

I'm often having to tell my son, "Tell Daddy about what happened with your friend at school today" or, "show daddy your new toy." Similarly, his dad will often encourage him to share news with me or tell me about the movie they have been watching. This positive interaction models a healthy relationship for our son.

Sure, there may be days where we disagreed on an issue or we may really just not feel like talking to each other, but we do it for our son. Five or ten minutes out of our day, to make our son happy, is the foremost priority. This certainly didn't happen overnight. It has taken years of practice and commitment. With the right boundaries in place though, we seem to make it work.

However, some clients of mine don't have such a flexible approach to communication. That's okay, too. Some parents need a clear idea of timing and require firm rules. I know that some families implement a call schedule where they speak to their child by phone every second night they are apart.

Some parents go as far as having set call times. This might be when the child wakes up or just before bed. Some parents even need rules, such as leaving the phone with their child in a private room to ensure there is no interference from the other parent. This is fine too.

As I say, you have the power to set your own needed rules and boundaries to make communication as effective as possible.

CHAPTER 3:

Two Sets of Everything, New Rules, and Road Mapping Schedules

Navigating Two Homes

I t's a strange feeling waking up alone every day in a bed you used to share with the person you loved. That immediate urge to say good morning is replaced with the fear of the unknown and the dread of facing another day on your own having to explain your new situation.

Some might say, "You don't need to explain yourself. Go live life proudly and independently." I don't disagree. This is your chance to thrive from your new independence, to recreate the life you always wanted, and to take charge.

At the same time, however, the reality is that you do have some explaining to do. This comes in the form of telling your children's school and practitioners and other professionals so that your children don't have to. There is nothing worse for a child than being put in that awkward situation where, for whatever reason, they are left explaining their parents' separation to their class teacher or after-school care provider.

Telling the School and Other Providers

When is the right time to tell the school or your local general practitioner about your divorce or separation? The simple answer is that there is never a right time. The best time is when you are ready. Practically though, it is generally a good time to spill the beans when the more significant changes have taken place, such as one parent moving out and when your children start living between two homes.

I had friends who have continued living in the same home with their ex, albeit separated, for years. They swear black and blue their children have no idea and think all is normal at home. I find this hard to believe. I don't know that children benefit from seeing their parents day in and day out sleeping in separate bedrooms and socializing separately.

One night they might have dinner with mom, and the next, dad. They don't see their parents lovingly interact as an intact couple. I see the obvious benefit of stability at home, but at the same time, I question the overall benefit to kids living this way.

I cannot comment which way is better. I am also definitely not here to preach mine or any other person's way as ideal. We all do as best we can in a difficult, life-changing situation. I do, however, believe that there is benefit to children who see parents happy, healthy, and living life as best they can.

If this means living apart but maintaining a sense of normalcy and business-like positivity at changeovers and during communication, I still do think this is better. Surely, there is some benefit to children learning to adapt and learning resilience? What do you believe?

I also completely understand the nervousness that comes with having to tell people outside of your inner circle what is going on at home. We all feel a little shame or guilt, right or wrong. However, most of the time, we didn't choose the separation. If we did, it's our choice and something we decided to better our life. People may talk. Let them.

Will there be the occasional town gossip who spreads rumors? Maybe so. Does it matter? I think not. What matters is that you feel confident and that you are doing what is best for you and for your family.

Irrespective of what other people may think of you, you are the person living your life. You are the person waking up each day, getting out of bed, and doing what you can to keep going and to lead by example for your wonderful children. You are the person in charge of your life and in charge of your future. So, go out there and tell the people who need to know, and ignore the ones who don't. Ignore the gossip, the stories, and the judging looks. You've got this.

This said, for several reasons, there is a fundamental need for your child's school to have an idea of what's going on at home. One important reason is so the school can best manage home communication. Another reason is to safely and effectively manage school pick-ups or calls to parents when a child becomes sick at school.

The most important reason is so your child's school can proactively and sensitively manage your child's emotions both in the classroom and also on the playground. Some children will need their teacher to look in on them a little more often. Teachers will also need to be more sensitive around tasks and homework.

Parents need to remember that during an emotionally challenging time such as a divorce, where children's lives become a moving feast of change and unpredictability, going to school each day will be a child's one constant. Even when their home and bedroom might change, when the days they get to see each parent will continue to shift and develop, and when life feels like a big experiment trying to determine what is best for them, children will go to school day in and day out.

They will share lunchtimes with their friends, seek guidance from their teacher, and maintain a sense of routine and regularity once inside the school gates. Sometimes even just the first breath they take as their backpack comes off and they settle into their school day helps your child to feel safe, free, and protected. This is the place they know, where things don't constantly change, where there is no parental conflict, and where they just get to feel like themselves.

For these very reasons, telling your child's school is a *must* during the early stages of separation. What does involving the school look like?

A written communication is often the best way. If you feel comfortable enough copying in your co-parent, that is even better. Remember, this is not your opportunity to share a *War and Peace* style exposition on the ins and outs of who cheated or why your marriage broke down. Rather, it is your opportunity to let the school know of your separation, any change in living arrangements, suggest ways they can be there for your child, and provide contact details for both parents. Below are a few tips.

- Elect for schools to provide any communication (emails, calls, newsletter, invitations, etc.) to both parents. The reason for this is to avoid the blame-game down the track. If your child's school is informing each of you about parent nights, award ceremonies, concerts, and the like, you cannot be blamed later for not advising your co-parent. Both of you have the responsibility of checking communication and staying informed. This is one way of minimizing future conflict and proactively engage in your child's schooling. When a child knows both their parents are aware of their upcoming school play, they don't have the underlying anxiety that one parent hasn't told the other (or won't), or that they have that responsibility. Ease the burden on your children where you can and provide them with this small comfort.

- Ask for help. Don't be afraid of being honest with your child's school if you are going through a hard time. This might be with respect to school fees, needing two sets of uniforms, struggling with being on time for school drop-off or pick-up, or dealing with a defiant child who is struggling with significant change.
- Be upfront about children who are struggling. Remember to reach out to the school counselor. Some children hate this. They feel embarrassed knowing other people are aware of their home problems. But the school counselor is often the best person to look out for your child and be their source of emotional support in coping with such change (We chat later about coping with a child who acts out during a divorce and delve into how best to manage children who play each parent off the other). In times like this, your school is often equipped with the best resources to manage these difficulties. It is also essential that parents and the school are on the same page and work together to assist when a child is suffering post separation.

My experience was a little different. My son wasn't at school when I separated. I did, however, wake up most mornings panicked by the thought of having to face my new reality. How was I, at such a young age and a thriving professional, having my world fall apart around?

As the days and weeks went on though, I cared less and less about what people might think and slowly felt more comfortable with my feelings (of being uncomfortable). Sure, life seemed like it was being turned upside down and I had to tell people almost daily "We've separated" and, "We are living apart now." But there was beauty in the unknown and in the possibilities that came with recreating what life was going to be. And oh how beautiful life has become since that time.

I remember waking up one morning, having a long shower, washing my hair, doing a blow-out, and putting on a new work outfit. I sat at my laptop and took charge of letting the important people in our son's life know what was going on. I wrote to our son's general practitioner to let them know that any future reports or results should be copied to both of us. I updated our health cover and changed details with required government bodies. I then emailed our son's childcare director and advised them of which days each of us were going to do pick-up or drop-off. I also changed our emergency contacts with the center (and included two people from each of our families).

Putting into writing what our parenting arrangements were going to be was a difficult and almost surreal experience. It was only the early days. Were these arrangements going to be in place on a permanent basis? What if hiccups occurred? How were we going to negotiate what the best arrangements might be for a (then) one-year-old?

These are the same questions I have faced when meeting with my clients (being a family and divorce lawyer) over the years. They ask questions such as, "How can we lock in parenting arrangements now for our toddler when there are so many years ahead?" "What if one of us moves?" "What happens when we re-partner and what if our new partner has kids too?"

"The truth is, unless you let go, unless you forgive yourself, unless you forgive the situation, unless you realize that the situation is over, you cannot move forward."
—**Steve Maraboli**

Historically, I have had more clients come to me separating when their children were in their early teens. Parenting arrangements came more naturally. Parents were guided by their children's wishes and what was practical. Sure, I have had my fair share of litigated court matters where parents are asking a judge to decide what arrangements would be better for their child. Will it be an equal time arrangement? Will dad only get alternate weekends? Each family is different and I have seen (almost!) everything.

Going through it yourself, however, is an entirely different experience. Perhaps this has made me a better lawyer? Can I now see how difficult it is for parents to come to a decision about where their child will live? With my lawyer hat on, there certainly are times I think, "Come on, are we seriously arguing over one night or which day you will change over?"

Now though, with my little one in mind, it's an extremely hard decision. A little piece of you breaks every time you say bye to your child and have a few days off from the parenting role. As a parent, you genuinely worry about how every decision you make will impact your child's life now and into the future. It may seem like a small, insignificant decision to make, but how does it then influence your little one?

The Hardest Part: Deciding on Parenting Arrangements and Remembering the Children's Best Interests Are Paramount

When determining what your post separation parenting arrangements should be, remember that your child's interests are paramount. That concept often sounds like legal jargon. It is. At the same time though, it makes a great deal of sense.

For example, whilst to most parents, driving one and a half hours after a school day to arrive to one parent's home might seem like not much of a big deal, think about how you would feel after a long day at school, sitting in a car for that long, still needing to do your homework, eat dinner, and unwind before another big day at school tomorrow. You then need to hop back in the car for another one and a half hours to get back to school the next morning. In making any decision, be sure to put yourself in your child's shoes and really think about how the decision may impact them.

Another example is to really think about how important an event is to a child. Parents often find themselves spending significant legal costs arguing about things from a child's attendance at a family function to spending one extra hour with the other parent each week. Is the end result to benefit the parent or the child?

Will the additional one hour really make a difference? Is it that important that your child attend your cousin's wedding? Rather than use your child as a topic for debate, think deeply about how much better it would be for them if their parents could be flexible and put their interests first. So, what types of things do you need to consider when coming up with a parenting plan?

Decision-making: In Australia, we call this *parental responsibility*. This is usually to do with the more important long-term issues including education, religion, change of name, medical decisions, and the like.

Parental time or living arrangements: Who will your child live with, and when? Some children live with both parents equally. This might be one week on and one week off. Alternatively, you might be like me and share your week. We change over on a Wednesday and switch back in one week on a Saturday morning and the other week on a Sunday night. This way, each of has a weekend with and without our son, and we share the week day responsibilities and care.

Other children don't live with their parents equally. Some kids live with mom and see dad on alternate weekends. Other kids might live with their dad and visit mom on weekends or holidays if she lives in another town. There is no perfect or right arrangement. Each family is so unique. What is important though, is ensuring that the arrangement works best for your child.

Special occasions and celebrations: Will your parenting plan consider what will happen on your child's birthday? On their parents' birthdays? How about Christmas and Easter? Most people also like to plan for occasions such as Mother's Day and Father's Day, Thanksgiving, Passover, Hanukkah, Diwali, Holi, Eid, New Year's Eve/Day, Lunar New Year, and cultural events.

School holiday arrangements: Will your usual parenting arrangements continue during the school holidays or differ? Some kids live with their parents week on, week off during the holidays. Others spend half the holidays with each parent. School holiday arrangements should consider travel (particularly if families live across the country or even internationally).

Extra-curricular activities: How will parents decide on what activities children participate in? Can both parents attend games or events? Give some thought to this one to minimize future conflict.

Permissions: Will you both be able to access information about your child? Most parenting plans include something to the effect that both parents be authorized to speak to and receive information and reports from treating medical practitioners, schools, and other professionals. This is a vital part of the co-parenting relationship. It assists both parents to be fully informed about their child and relieves pressure from parents having to pass on information. This also helps reduce conflict.

Travel: Now this is a huge one. Deciding on what guidelines you put around interstate and international travel is so important. I always advise my clients that although it is difficult to let go and agree to let your child travel with their other parent, there is so much benefit to encouraging your children to see other parts of your country and even the world. To help facilitate safe travel, it is always important to establish guidelines and rules. It is common for parenting plans (and even Court orders) to include provisions around travel. These can include parents sharing itineraries, copies of airline tickets, details about accommodation, and rules around travel to countries that are not signatories to the *Hague Convention on the Civil Aspects of International Child Abduction*.

Electronic communication: Some families are able to be flexible and encourage regular electronic communication. Other families who are more high conflict prefer to have set times parents can call their children when with the other parent.

So, what do I do? This is a question I am asked almost daily. It is important to remember that what works for me and my co-parent will be completely different to another family. Each family is unique. Each set of co-parents are unique. Children have their own unique needs, personalities, and developmental requirements. What works for my three-year-old likely won't work for another three-year-old.

Although I will share what works well for me at the moment, please know that it doesn't mean you should implement what I do, or that what I am doing now will continue to work in five years' time. Above all else, what I do know is that I need to be flexible, open to change, and realistic in my approach. This is particularly true given that we separated so long ago and when our son was so young.

The arrangements that suit my now three-year-old will need revisited when he starts primary school and high school. Things will change when he starts having weekend sports and when he forms a group of friends as he grows older. Things will change again when he gets his first girlfriend and wants to spend his weekends at the movies and concerts, not sitting with mom and her girlfriends at cafés or playing at the local play center.

To be frank, the reality of life is that we will experience ongoing changes, new partners, blended families, and maybe even stepsiblings. As parents, we need to be open to navigating these changes. I often work with clients where emotions are raw and conflict is high. Two years into litigation, one or both parents have re-partnered and sometimes they are expecting again with their new partner. Things get messy and there are so many significant life changes. But the reality is that all of these new factors and circumstances need to be taken into account.

My parenting plan . . . We use a fortnightly routine for our living arrangements. We ended up moving to suburbs within close proximity to each other, our son's pre-school, and our places of work.

Week one: With me from 6 p.m. Sunday to 6 p.m. Wednesday. With his dad from 6 p.m. Wednesday to 6 p.m. Sunday.

Week two: With me from 9 a.m. Saturday to 6 p.m. Wednesday. With his dad from 6 p.m. Wednesday to 9 a.m. Saturday.

What I love about our living arrangements is that our son shares half the week with each parent. We feel this is a good amount of time between changeovers. Given he was so young when this routine started, he doesn't spend too long away from either parent.

We have been as flexible as possible with this routine. We do not always stick to the times. Some Sundays he might come home at 4:30 p.m. and other Sundays it might be 8 p.m. if he or I have been away. Wednesday times shift depending on work arrangements and our plans. If there are weekends either of us have something going on or we are away, we are generally flexible with swapping weekends or giving the other parent the first "right of care" if we are going to have our son sleep with his grandparents.

Don't get me wrong. I think that there is nothing more beautiful than encouraging the strong bond between a child and their grandparents. At the same time though, we value that we each have little time with our son. If we are going to be away, we do offer each other additional time before then reaching out to our respective parents to help out.

What does flexibility look like for us? We use SMS as our primary means of communication to chat about changeovers and arrangements. On Wednesdays, we are regularly in contact to see how each of our days are going and what time will suit best for a changeover. My son's dad works in his office on Wednesdays, which is my work from home or parenting day. Similarly, on weekends, we text on the morning of a changeover to discuss the best timing. We are both realistic that things come up and a set time is not always the easiest.

There have been times when each of us want to travel internationally without our son. We have been accommodating and able to care for our son, with the help of our parents, during thess periods. I even reached out to my son's father's parents to offer them some extra time with their grandson during these times.

It is hard to open a line of communication with people you no longer see or speak to, but I acknowledge how important it is for my son to see me communicate with and be in the presence of other members of his family. I remember at a changeover with my son's grandparents when his father was overseas. I observed how something as simple as saying *"Hello, how are you?"* to my former mother-in-law, in the presence of my son, brought a big smile to his face. I remember when I collected him from her home, he immediately said to me when we got into the car, *"Mamma, you know my* yiayia*?"* (Greek for grandmother). Despite everyone's differences, I responded straight away, *"Of course I do. You are so lucky to have so many people in your live who love you, baby."*

The importance of this exchange isn't to suggest I am best of friends with my ex's family, or even him. But it is to reinforce the importance of the messages you send your child. Children hear and see everything. There is no point talking the talk but having your actions show something the complete opposite. Try as best you can to put your differences aside, to shield your child from conflict, and to model what healthy adult relationships look like. Trust me, you will thank yourself for this in the future.

What works for other parents? Other common parenting schedules I recommend and have experienced through my work, include the following:

A week on and a week off with each parent. Changeovers usually occur on a Friday after school to allow children to settle over the weekend and then ease back into the school week before changing homes.

A 2/2/3 arrangement. Monday/Tuesday with one parent, Wednesday/Thursday with the other parent, and then alternate weekends (Friday/Saturday/Sunday).

Where it's not an equal time arrangement, many parents implement a 9/5 arrangement. Week one: With one parent Monday through Thursday and with the other parent Thursday through Monday. Week two: Live with one parent and spend one weekday overnight with the other parent.

Use this space to map out what arrangement you think will work best for you:

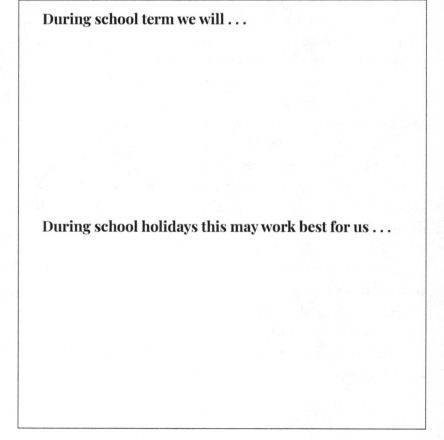

During school term we will . . .

During school holidays this may work best for us . . .

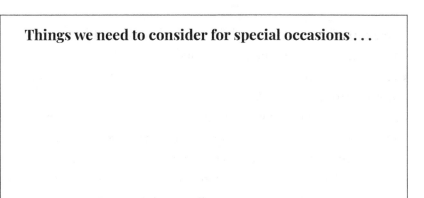

At the end of the day, you need to determine which arrangements work best for you and your family. Some parents are unable to accommodate an equal time arrangement because of work commitments or living too far apart. Other parents need to factor in their children's special needs, a parent's mental health or a history of family violence. It is important to feel comfortable with your arrangements and agree to a plan that best benefits your children and provides stability, consistency, and routine.

The Need for Routine and Stability: What Works and What Doesn't

People often ask why consistency and routine are so important. As much as I promote being adaptable to change and flexible with arrangement, consistency is still imperative to a child's development and long-term wellbeing. Knowing which parent a child will live with over various days each week is important for a child's sense of security and safety.

It will, of course, take time to become familiar with new living arrangement, but by having a stable pattern of care in place, you free your child from confusion, feelings of displacement, and provide them with protection. It is common knowledge across social science professionals that children do best in stable households. This does not mean staying married just so that your child can experience an intact, stable family, but rather, providing stability amongst two households.

Having a consistent parenting plan provides children with a clear expectation of how to feel and what to expect day-to-day. Too many transitions between homes cause stress and often encourage feelings of loss of control. This can negatively impact a child's school and academic behavior, mental health, and ability to maintain friendships and relationships. A clear parenting plan or set of Court Orders encourages parents to be co-operative and takes out the need for too many last-minute decisions. Parenting plans promote stability, teamwork, and amiability. This provides a child with a unified approach to being part of a separated family.

My client Melanie had a difficult time with a lack of routine and consistency in the early days following her separation. She tried bird nesting initially (where parents take turns living in the house with the child). This created false expectations in her child. Her daughter remained reliant on both parents to be there all the time and could not differentiate what was happening because they all remained living in the same home.

When her ex-husband had his off week, her daughter would be inconsolable. It was like losing him all over again each fortnight. This caused all sorts of behavioral issues, acting out, and school refusal. As they slowly moved to a more consistent and regular routine with only Melanie living at home, and her ex finding his own place, their daughter slowly came to appreciate her new environment and was better able to cope with the separation.

She had time with mom in the old family home, and treasured the time she spent with her dad at his new place. At first, they had a very flexible arrangement with no real pattern of care. After a few months of time, the cracks started to show again. Their daughter became overwhelmed and confused. She was having trouble at school. Their child psychologist recommended a more stable pattern of care (three nights/four nights with each parent), so that their daughter knew where she would be and when. This helped her cope with ongoing change, take care of her belongings, plan homework, and generally feel comfortable again with day-to-day tasks and life.

My son is only just about to turn four. He seems to have, however, worked out that Wednesday means changeover. Every morning, he will wake up and ask me, "*What day is it today?*. When I say Monday or Tuesday, he knows it's a pre-school day. This excites him. When I say Wednesday, he knows it's his day to change homes and I see that this also excites him.

By being prepared for this, he is better able to regulate his expectations and emotions. On weekends, he knows Saturdays mean swimming lessons with his dad. On Sundays, he knows it's movie night with mom.

At what age though, is it time to re-evaluate your parenting arrangements? Is there ever a right time or right age? With Court Orders, there is an expectation that the orders remain in place generally until a child is eighteen (at least in Australia). This is unless two parents can agree otherwise.

I have definitely seen my fair share of parents ending up back in Court five to ten years later, when orders have been made for infants. The reality is that with time, life changes. Where a parent may have expected their child to go to high school might have evolved. Employment changes, people move suburbs, families blend, and children grow up and develop. Children all go through puberty, and teenagers want their voices heard. How parents deal with this will be very much dependent upon their co-parenting relationship.

The higher conflict the relationship, the more difficult accepting change and allowing flexibility might seem. I certainly do not think that just because children grow older, this means you need to completely throw out your routine of parenting arrangements. It might mean, however, that you need to revisit what works.

Take me, for example. Right now, a changeover every few days works well for our little one. As he grows and starts high school, makes friends, and has afternoon sport and activities, such frequent changeovers might be more inconvenient than helpful. A week-long routine with one parent might work better.

With a week arrangement, I can do soccer or tennis training one week and his dad can attend the week after. We can share weekend games one week each (or both go if we are comfortable with that). Re-shifting how we think and what we do takes effort, but it can mean a more consistent lifestyle and a happier child. We need to be open and cognizant of the fact that what works now may not have longevity, but the practices we establish and the way we do things will. What do I mean by that?

By learning open and respectful communication in the early days and by having an established set of boundaries in your co-parenting relationship, changes to day-to-day living arrangements and routines won't be as difficult. People often adapt and cope better with change when their more entrenched practices are well developed. Keep the fundamentals the same and your co-parenting life will flourish.

Co-Parenting Fundamentals: Same Rules, Different Homes

Just as stability of living arrangements is important, so too is consistency amongst households in terms of rules, expectations, and boundaries. Even though you and your co-parent may have your differences, working together and encouraging consistent approaches to guidelines, schedules, and routines are important for children.

Although the exact rules amongst two homes do not have to be identical, with generally consistent frameworks, children aren't confused and displaced by navigating two completely different homes with different disciplinary environments. What do I mean when I talk about disciplinary environments and rules?

- School routine
- Homework
- Use of electronics and devices
- Curfew
- Activities which are permitted and others which are not
- Language and swearing
- Food restrictions (views on junk food or treats)
- Use of public transport
- Sleep overs with friends
- Piercings

These may not be topics you necessarily want to have rules or boundaries in place for, but it is often good to establish consistency in parental expectations to avoid children playing their parents off one another. In my work, I often experience parents purposefully having opposing views on these types of issues to try to win over their child. I have experienced many parents allowing piercing or tattoos, allowing a later curfew, and being more relaxed on homework and study to encourage their child to spend more time with them and to be more defiant with their other parent.

These scenarios often arise in families who are high conflict and parents who continue to traverse a toxic relationship. This dynamic is incredibly difficult to navigate and often requires the intervention of a specialized professional such as a family therapist or parenting coordinator.

My client Melanie struggled with this in the early stages of separation. Her daughter was allowed unlimited screen time at dad's house. Dad allowed chocolate brownies for breakfast on the way to school, and spoiled their daughter with Sephora makeup, unlimited H&M shopping sprees, and the latest iPhone every time it came out. Melanie had different rules at her home.

No screen time on school days. Her daughter had to save up and budget to shop for luxuries. I think the biggest blunder, however, was buying her adolescent daughter a flip phone for her birthday knowing all the kids were using an iPhone. This doesn't make Melanie a bad parent. It is, however, a good example of needing to navigate the differences in parenting styles when going through a separation.

Each parent is welcome to have their own way of doing things, and will likely have different values, morals, and life views. Some parents encourage the use of modern technology, others avoid it. Some moms are into girly clothes and makeup, others prefer to focus on being outdoors and in nature. Parents often come to me during a separation, confused and upset about why these things matter. I always say that during the early days, children will find it extraordinarily confusing to navigate two homes and two sets of rules/boundaries.

Children will test limits and likely gravitate to the parent who seems more relaxed and gives them more, materially speaking. As difficult as it is, by trying to meet midway and agreeing to a mutual set of rules in both households (that considers each of your ways of thinking and parenting styles) your child will likely benefit more. Where there are not two different options, children will see that each parent offers something similar. This takes pressure off parents and also off children.

It might mean that you have to give in to a little screen time, or allow your child that belly piercing you are so against, but it will also mean a calmer, more stable home. At the same time though, don't give in to big issues or topics which are completely against your morals and what you want in your child and for your family. Stability and keeping the peace are important, but so too is your right to raise your child as you wish.

If you are dealing with a co-parent who purposefully creates inconsistencies amongst your households, do not fight back. Do not give up on your expected guidelines at home just to win back your child. There may be periods of debate and argument with your children as they get older. You may feel like you are the stricter or tougher parent. But by being a consistent parent and modeling consistent behaviors, your child will benefit in the long run.

Children often end up returning to the home that promotes safety, security, and protection in the form of consistency. Sure, your teenager might hate you for a week for grounding them or taking away their laptop or phone, but the lack of routine at their other parent's home will end up causing them to crave and need the security you provide. Trust me. All children need consistency. This helps them to navigate the real world and make better choices. Lack of structure creates poor decision making and leads to increased stress.

If there are ongoing issues amongst two households, you can discuss with your co-parent the benefits of maintaining structure across your homes. What does this involve? Showcase for your co-parent how much easier their life will be by promoting structure and consistent routine. You will find that by knowing their own lifestyle will improve, they will become more accommodating of what you are suggesting.

By implementing a similar wake up time in the morning and similar expectations of what is required of your child in the morning (bath and hygiene routine, breakfast, preparation of school bags, getting dressed and the time to leave), mornings become less chaotic and parents feel less stress. Leaving on time and getting to work on time becomes more achievable.

Dinner and night routines can be easier if you both maintain consistent schedules. Aim to implement a reliable pick-up time. Have the same rules in place about dinner options, what is required of your child for cleaning up/packing away, and encourage the same nightly bath and bed routine. For younger children, this might mean encouraging the same bedtime set up, reading the same books, and having the same white noise or music playing.

For older children, encourage similar amounts of TV or iPad time. Promote a similar view about homework and study. In turn, dinner and nights become slower, easier, and your time is freed up for parent time. You will soon find you are having more good days that terrible ones.

When we talk about routine, stability, consistency, and living arrangements, we also need to think about how we can make our children's lives easier when they move from house to house. What does this entail? I believe there is such importance in having consistency in changeovers and making your child's life easier when it comes to packing, belongings, and living out of two homes.

Some parents have a structure where a child only has one set of clothes/shoes, and transports these from house to house. This creates, in my view, an added area of dispute and conflict. Socks will go missing, jumpers may shrink in the dryer, and kids will naturally have falls and rip their pants. Is a parent to blame? Will a child feel to blame? Why put the additional pressure on a child by giving them the responsibility of ensuring their clothes and shoes go safely between homes?

I had a client whose son would save pocket money just to buy spare undies and socks from the local store to take between households to prevent his parents from arguing. He had been exposed to so much yelling and frustrating about missing clothing, and he felt responsibile for the arguments. My heart hurt for this little boy who was just trying to keep the peace. Instead of saving his money for games or outings with friends, he was pressured into keeping the peace amongst his parents.

I had another client whose daughter was adamant that every Sunday before she changed homes, she would do all the washing and drying of her uniforms and sports clothes to save her parents from arguing over why clothes came home dirty. One parent was forgetting to wash the school uniform after pick-up on a Friday and returning it home on a Sunday needing a wash before school on Monday. I get it. Incredibly frustrating.

Rather than watch her parents fight, she would wash and dry her school dresses, pack them into her bag, and head back to her other parent's on a Sunday night, fuss free. The angry text messages and phone calls on a Sunday evening ceased. But the pressure this poor young girl was feeling was unimaginable.

I find it easiest for each parent to have their own clothes, underwear, shoes, etc., at home. Two sets of uniforms (where affordable) also makes life easier and saves an argument. No parent should be reliant upon the other parent to dress their child. Make it exciting for your child. Go on a bi-annual shopping trip. Let your child pick out a few outfits and encourage them to dress themselves in the morning. At the same time though, be realistic. Children will need to transport some items back and forth on changeover day. What I find works best for me is to dress my son in an outfit on changeover day to his dad, and his dad will often dress him in those same clothes when he returns a few days later.

That way, we ensure clothes are returned. We are also realistic. Some of dad's clothes will stay in my laundry basket for days (or weeks!) but when it comes to folding, I keep a spare bag in his room where I pile his dad's clothes, undies, shoes and return them. I won't lie . . . there has been the occasional time my son's dad has chased me up for losing a jumper or good pair of pants. They usually have just been sitting in my clean clothes basket for a while. I am a lazy folder, so I avoid the clean clothes basket for weeks on end!

Similar to clothing, kids will often be excited to pack their toys or games with them when changing homes. Some parents loathe this. Again, I get it. You are spending your hard-earned money on a toy or a game, and there is a good chance it might not come back. At the same time though, you make your child happy and encourage peace in their life by allowing them to take that toy or game to their other parent.

For my son, it's toy cars. I cannot tell you how many Hot Wheels cars we have lying around. Monster trucks? Even more. Every Wednesday, without fail, he goes into his bedroom and starts picking which cars and trucks he wants to take to his dads. Sometimes I get them back. Other times I don't. I do not let this worry me. There are bigger life stressors to focus on. There are also plenty of occasions when one of his dad's toy cars or Lego sets ends up at my home. It's all part of being a collaborative co-parent, right?

CHAPTER 4:

Who Is Boss?
Healthy Decision Making

Sharing Parental Responsibility and Decision Making:
Learning to Agree Despite the Differences

You are probably thinking by now, "She makes it all sound so simple. Just learn to get on with your co-parent. Do things together. But really, it's not that easy."

Trust me, I get that it is not that easy. I know that on most occasions, you will want to rip out your co-parent's hair, scream across the room, and tell the world how difficult your co-parent is. No part of life was created to be easy, and no human is perfect. I certainly am not perfect. There are days when even if I am getting on well with my co-parent, I want to scream and shout because we just cannot agree on a really simple issue.

Examples of this have included agreeing on the right time to get rid of our son's dummy, getting on the same page about toilet training, and being consistent with naps and bedtimes. The reality is, we share our son equally. We both have the responsibility of jointly making the big-ticket decisions such as vaccinations, choice of school, and religious upbringing. But what happens when we just cannot come to an agreement? Who gets the final say and how do we get there? How do we reach resolution?

In sitting down to write this book, and in particular this chapter, I thought a lot about the decision-making process. For parents, decisions can evolve into a competition of competing ideas and a fight to be right and come out on top.

But does it really matter who won the final decision? Does it really matter that you had to give in about which school your child goes to? Are you trying to find a difference of opinion simply to debate? Are you causing controversy just to continue the conflict? Isn't the reality of parenting that you and your co-parent share a common purpose, the goal of raising resilient, passionate, humble, and ambitious children of the future?

"Children deserve both parents. They deserve to know that their parents respect each other if nothing else. So that really helps me set the standard of how I try and behave."

—**Jewel Kilcher**

And so really, should not the real focus be on the ability to make decisions collaboratively to model the ability to effectively communicate? Who really cares if you ended up having the last say? Your co-parent might the worst person on the planet. They may have cheated on you for years. They may have gambled away a big savings account. They may be a pretty bad person. But would it not be better for your child to see you jointly make decisions about their future, rather than bickering away and forever making them part of a conflict dynamic?

My client, Samantha, and her ex-husband, Rodger, were in a very high conflict relationship. Following their separation, they continued living in the same home. This made matters worse. When it came to discussing and making decisions about schooling, although they had previously decided which high school their boys would attend, following their separation, this decision became a cause of absolute grief.

Legal letter after legal letter, they debated why one parent should have the sole decision-making power about this issue. The reality was that they both still wanted their boys to go to the school they had initially chosen, but they were more interested in arguing than in making a collaborative decision to best serve their children.

This only caused detriment to their boys, who became caught up in the conflict. The boys were involved in choosing sides, listening to their parents complain about the other, and even started involving themselves in screaming matches amongst their parents in the kitchen. Not ideal at all.

Sometimes the toughest part about being a family lawyer, and having been through a separation myself, is battling the internal battle of what a lawyer would advise their client with what a separated mom wants to tell their client about the reality of the situation. These days, I find myself diving in and out of the lawyer and mom hat and testing scenarios for my clients.

I told Samantha that it was time to get over the conflict, to shape up as a parent, and let go of decisions that weren't as important. I advised her to think long-term about her boys and the impact the conflict had on them, as opposed to which parent might win the decision.

This also got me thinking about how children handle the experience of growing up with separated parents making decisions for them. We all like to think that if we do it right, if we maintain a cordial and collaborative relationship with our co-parent, our children won't be affected by having separated parents. The reality is that they will be affected and they will experience differences and challenges. However, the way we go about modeling and exposing them to the decision-making process will change how they are affected and how they cope with change into their adulthood.

Another client of mine, Rachel, found herself in a position where she was able to reach agreement with her ex on most decisions, but when it came to medical issues, they simply could not see eye to eye. Her husband was dead against any form of naturopathic treatment for their children, whereas she was a strong believer of alternate therapies, particularly for their son who suffered from bad eczema and allergies. Every medical issue turned into contested litigation and arguments became bigger and bigger.

Ultimately, and with years of family therapy, they came to an agreement. They would be required as parents to consult on issues and Rachel would be required to obtain her ex's views on a medical issue. But if an agreement could not be reached, she would have the final decision-making power in relation to medical issues. This was what was needed to move forward and avoid spending the next ten years in court fighting over every issue that came their way. They both compromised.

They sought external help, participated in therapy, pushed through the immediate desire to fight and argue, and finally looked to the bigger picture and what was best for their family.

There are various types of decision-making responsibility. Although different countries and jurisdictions use different terminology, there are three main ways parents make decisions following separation:

- Joint or equal decision-making responsibility: Both parties are responsible for coming together and reaching a joint decision.

- Sole parental or decision-making responsibility: Although parents may consult or take on the opinion of the other, one parent has the final say.
- Parallel decision-making responsibility: This concept works well in separated families where you both understand the importance of each having a role in the decision-making process but know you will not be able to reach a joint decision. Instead, each parent is given responsibility for different topics. One parent may decide on school and health and the other may decide on religion.

Obviously, it is not always possible to make joint decisions. Consideration of where responsibility will fall must come down to your family dynamics. Where there has been family violence, coercive control, or extreme toxicity in the parental relationship, consideration really needs to be given to sole parental decision-making.

I recently finished a five-day parenting trial where I acted for the mother in a high conflict separation characterized by a long history of family violence and trauma. Dad sought court orders to share responsibility with mom over all the major decisions for their children: school, health, religion, and more. This was in the context of a five-year period of separation where every single decision was an argument, boundaries were crossed, and dad was unable to acknowledge the violence he had perpetrated and the impact that had on the family.

Ultimately, sole decision-making power was given to mom, as it would simply not be safe or conducive to a healthy dynamic for these two parents to continue being in communication or making decisions together.

Bubs and Minors: The Road Ahead

It used to be less common for parents who had babies or toddlers to separate. Being divorced with a baby was almost unheard of (unless the other parent had taken off). These days, parents are more easily see the negative impact that conflict in a household has on children.

More so, parents are deciding that separation might be better with young children who may not entirely remember their parents being together. I cannot comment on whether this is the right or wrong approach. I certainly took this view when separating when my son was one.

He may remember his parents together, and he might be more accepting and understanding of living in two households. After all, he has now spent more of his life living across two homes than one. I am, however, noticing more and more that as he gets older and has become increasingly inquisitive and talkative, that he is trying to understand why he has two homes, why his mom and dad don't live together, and why his family is different to some of the other families at school.

Co-parent decision making has a huge impact for babies and young children. Every decision we make will influence their learning, development, and ability to regulate emotions. Young children are unable to voice their needs. Reliance is placed on parents and caregivers to identify what is required and actively model appropriate relationships, communication, and decision making.

When navigating decision-making for bubs and young children, what are the sorts of things to consider?

Breast feeding versus bottle feeding (pumped breast milk or formula): There is no right or wrong approach, and rather than debating the science behind breast milk or formula milk, parents need to try to come together and determine what will be best for their child. It might be that mom can pump milk to provide to dad to feed during his time with the child. Dad's time with the child may be more frequent periods of shorter duration with the child to allow mom to continue breast feeding.

Routine: Routine for naps, sleeping times, dummy's, choice of nappies, creams, and comforters matter. Although these little things might seem harmless or irrelevant, being on the same page and making joint decisions about a child's routine is imperative to their sense of familiarity and security with both parents.

Toileting: Parents of infant children who are yet to be toilet trained need to be on the same page when deciding to potty train. Both parents will need to be involved and implement similar arrangements at their homes to make the process easiest for the child. We know that stability is required for a child when learning to independently use the toilet. Some good ideas are to purchase the same potty, agree on an approach to wearing undies during the day and at night, and to use the same terminology when referring to private parts and going to the bathroom. You might also both decide to use a reward system.

Attendance at daycare or pre-school: How many days will your child attend? Is your child too young to be left with strangers? This is a big decision that parents will often need to make together. There are so many benefits of early learning and care. Parents should be unified in their approach to attendance at centers. I can't think of anything worse for a child who is going through a separation than to also have to attend multiple centers during their week.

Use of media devices: Will you let your toddler use an iPad at restaurants and cafés? At what age is television time okay? This is really a day-to-day issue as opposed to a major long-term decision.

But nevertheless, it is good to have a joint approach with your co-parent to maintain consistency across households.

Medication and vaccinations: Minors have various government mandated vaccines. There are also other vaccines that are recommended by treating professionals but not necessitated by government. So, how do you reach decisions about what is needed, or not needed, with your co-parent? This is something that should be spoken about in early days. If a decision cannot be reached, it is often useful to garner the joint opinion of your child's practitioner. If you are still in a deadlock, use a good mediator or family therapist to resolve.

The School Years

Just when you think you have made all the important decisions for your child, overnight they will grow into bigger kids, teenagers, and young adults. Emotions will run high, you will find yourself debating not only your ex but also your child, and every decision seems like a major battle. I am a big believer in your parenting plan or set of Court Orders clearly setting out the decision-making process.

This should include how you make decisions, what the circuit breaker will be, and who gets the right of last say. It may seem like something you don't need if you get on well, but down the track, as the years pass, as people re-partner, and the journey of life faces roadblocks, you will be thankful you had that parenting plan in place. What types of issues might you have to consider with school-aged children?

Which school your child attends: This will include primary school, middle school, and high school. You will need to actively consider whether you prefer a public school, religious school, private school, or home schooling. You will also need to consider location and proximity to home and to family.

Extra-curricular activities: Will your children participate in one, three, or five activities? What happens when soccer falls in your time in one week but in your co-parent time the next week? Can you force your co-parent to take your child to the activity? What if you want your daughter to do ballet but your co-parent is entirely against dancing? These sorts of decisions will come up again and again during the school years. Being open to listen, take in opinions, consider, and then respond is so important. Try to always put yourself in your child's shoes.

Travel, holidays, and scheduling summer plans: I always think it is important to raise these issues and decide well in advance of intended travel plans. I like to think about my year ahead, and where possible, map out when I might want my child to take a holiday and where our usual parenting arrangements might clash. I then email my co-parent well ahead of any holidays or travel to let him know of my plans and to invite discussion about the issue.

Attendance at parties, sleepovers and events: What happens when one parent allows overnight sleepovers during primary school but the other parent thinks the child is too young? The best way of trying to overcome a difference in opinion here is to share your views with your co-parent and discuss implementation of joint guidelines or boundaries around the issue. For example, both parents will request information and updates from the sleepover host's parents. Another agreed rule might be no unisex sleepovers.

Use of technology and mobile phones: This one is coming up more and more frequently as our world develops. Should primary school-aged children have mobiles? Is there not a benefit to a child having a phone to contact their parents before and after school? Should a child have their own phone to contact the parent with whom they are not living? Could there be benefits in having an open line of communication between child and parent in the context of a separated family? At least it removes the need for you to always answer and speak with your former partner.

However, given the increased cyber security and child abuse risks with the online environment in this day and age, it is really important that both parents think about and decide on the use of a mobile phone or other electronic devices. It is useful to collaboratively decide on boundaries surrounding use of technology. Many of my clients share the iCloud account their child uses and share passwords for things like their child's email and social media accounts.

Navigating Planet Teenager: The Need for Consistency

Separated or not, the majority of parents will struggle parenting their teenager. Just as you are going through change, your teenager is experiencing a world of instability, stress, upset about the world, and ongoing change. Teenagers, above everyone else, need stability and co-operative parenting. Teenagers need to know they are loved and supported. Everything in their lives seems complicated and unfair.

For this reason, it is important that as co-parents you model healthy adult relationships and communication skills. Work together to show your teenager that their parents can be a team despite the divorce. Teenagers are constantly watching and learning. The way they communicate with other adults and friends will be largely dependent on what you as a parent model. So, what might you need to consider as separated parents with teenagers?

Drugs, alcohol and parties: Parents need to try to be on the same page about decisions involving social activities, use of alcohol, and attitude toward illicit substances. Unfortunately, these issues are becoming all too common in modern society and something co-parents really need to establish consistency in.

Attitudes toward university and college: Although this is a decision that your child needs to make, as a parent, you will have influence over how they reach their own decision. Nothing can be harder for a child than making a big decision about their future education and having their parents on different pages about what is best for them. Try to raise the issue with your co-parent and discuss your views, share opinions, and jointly decide how you will approach the topic with your child.

Sexual health and relationships: We were all teenagers once. At one point or another, our parents gave us the talk about the birds and the bees. Think about how beneficial it would be for your child to have their parents collaborating about the best way to approach teenage relationships and sex. Perhaps you can decide who will do the talk and who will more regularly check in.

Overseas travel and exchanges: Many schools offer cultural exchanges to overseas countries. I remember travelling to Italy when I was in grade eleven to help me better my Italian language skills before taking my final exams in high school. The opportunity was once in a lifetime and I gained so much from being with my family in Italy and experiencing the culture, the food, the people, and the language.

When teenagers are offered the opportunity to travel during high school, both parents need to agree on the final decision. Rather than use the power to decide something as special as overseas travel as a bribe or punishment, work collaboratively to discuss the advantages and disadvantages of the experience. Jointly put in place important rules and guidelines for your child when traveling. A united approach is always better received and the rules you jointly give your child are more likely to be followed if given by both parents.

Piercings and tattoos: Most countries don't allow children under eighteen-years-old to get piercings or tattoos without the permission of their parent. When children have separated parents, they are more likely to go to the lenient parent to obtain approval. This is one of those decisions that both parents should really be involved in and have an opportunity to discuss with their child.

Safe Zone for Opinions and Proposals

I have set out above some of the most common issues you will need to decide. You may however, find yourself in a place of battle about many of the major decisions that need to be made.

How do you go about identifying the decision, considering your co-parent's view, and then reaching an agreement? It is really important to be clear about what issue you need to resolve. What is the decision? How does the decision impact your child? What options are available? Is there a midpoint we can find? By improving your thinking and listening skills, you will make better decisions. Remove the emotion and focus on the issue at hand.

Too many of my clients ask me, "How can I take the emotion out of it? These are my children." They are right. Any decisions made about your children are important. But are your emotions taking over? Often, identifying what emotions you are experiencing at the time of a decision will help you to identify the best outcome. Sit back and think about what emotion you are experiencing, the context behind the emotion, and the overall goal you are trying to achieve. By identifying the outcome or end goal, your emotion will usually fall away.

The next important step is to understand and consider your options. You may have one opinion about a particular topic, but it is important to reflect on the opinion/s of your co-parent. Earlier this year, I was adamant about changing my son's pre-school. I felt so strongly about this that I could not see reason and ignored every opinion of my co-parent.

It wasn't until I slowed down to think about the repercussions of changing pre-schools and how that might impact my son, and allowed myself to really consider the decision, that I started considering my co-parents opinions. And, they were valid opinions.

> *"Nothing in life is more important than the ability to communicate effectively."*
> **—Gerald R. Ford,** former United States President

Had we considered his strong friendship circle? Would we be bombarding him with too much change too soon? Would a new school have the same problems? The current school was very local and easy to get to. Would a new school mean earlier wake ups and later arrival at home each evening? Lots to think about and lots to discuss.

By allowing myself to listen, reflect, and consider my co-parent's views, I ended up making a completely different decision and we did not change his school. I continue to look back on the conversations we had and think to myself, "Why couldn't I just have listened when he was trying to tell me his point of view? Was I being defiant or ignoring his opinion just so I could be right?" But, as they say, practice makes perfect, and you only learn from experience.

When any major, or even day-to-day, decision arises, and you need to try to reach a joint outcome, it is important to have a safe zone for the communication process. We talk a lot about communication in Chapter 2 of this book. Communication is paramount to effective decision making. It's important to provide guidance and support to your co-parent to encourage educated and cooperative decision-making.

When having a conversation about a big decision, think about whether what you are saying is going to help you achieve your goal. Are you being fair? Are you being open minded? Decision making brings with it great responsibility. As a parent, you are faced with responsibility every single day.

> *"Excellent communication doesn't just happen naturally. It is a product of process, skill, climate, relationship, and hard work."*
>
> **—Pat McMillan,** **author and CEO**

Creating a safe zone is about encouraging an open and protected forum for the discussion of ideas. This might be via a parenting application on your phone, text message or email, or even by sitting down across a table, sharing a meal, and floating ideas with each other. In a safe zone, both parents should feel comfortable sharing ideas, raising concerns, and jointly try to reach mutual decisions. The decision-making process is not an avenue to bring up past conflict, to denigrate, or to risk harm to the co-parenting relationship. The communication process should be used solely for the common purpose of deciding about the issue at hand.

Making Decisions with a Narcissistic Ex

If you have been co-parenting with a narcissist, much of what I have set out above won't apply. Narcissistic abuse makes it incredibly difficult to effectively make decisions with your co-parent and can have a detrimental effect on your own thoughts and ability to make decisions.

When it comes to making big decisions about long-term issues including school and health, your narcissistic co-parent may cause you to have self-doubt, suffer fear of noncompliance, feel isolated, or cause you to become increasingly dependent on them for guidance because you worry about making the wrong decision. I assume that if you are reading this book, you have separated and hopefully come to realize that unfortunately, you child's other parent is a narcissist. If this is the case, you have to be clever in your approach to co-parenting and joint decision making.

We know that co-parenting with a narcissist and making decisions with that person is complicated. Narcissistic parents are often more concerned with how a decision will impact them than how it will affect their child. Instead of prioritizing their child and placing their child's needs first, a narcissistic parent will care first and foremost about their needs and their image.

When making decisions with your narcissistic co-parent, make sure you maintain the boundaries we talked about above. Avoid situations where your co-parent is given the opportunity to act out in anger toward your child. Try to also avoid situations where you feel shamed, guilted, gaslit, or controlled by your co-parent because of the issue you have raised.

Relationships of this nature usually require very detailed decision-making guidelines and rules surrounding how you communicate, how you go about making decisions, and who has the final say. It is also important to have mandated dispute resolution mechanisms in place for times when you cannot reach a decision and are required to both consent to something (such as international travel or school). Document everything. Keep records. Block communication that becomes hostile, intimidating, or harassing.

CHAPTER 5:

It's the Messages You Send That Matter the Most

Painting a Picture of Your Ex:
There's Positivity in Peace

Funny enough, I sat down to work on this chapter of the book during Harmony Week at my son's school. This might only be an Australian tradition, but essentially, Harmony Week is a celebration that recognizes diversity and encourages inclusiveness, respect, and a sense of belonging for everyone.

My son's pre-school asked that families pack a photo of the family for show and tell. I panicked in one of those moments of guilt, shame, and sadness. Was my three-year-old going to have to tell the class all about his two families—his two homes? Would I send two photographs into school, one of my son, me, and my parents, and one of my son with his dad and paternal family? Or would I go back and find an old family photo from when my son was an infant? Was it even okay for me to go back and look at old family photos and share those memories with him? Or would that confuse him even more?

That night, as my son and I lay on the lounge preparing for the nightly bed routine, I pulled up some old albums on my laptop and scrolled through them. When old photos popped up of family celebrations with my son's dad pictured, my son immediately said, *"Why is Daddy here? He isn't in this family . . . he has his own family."* A little piece of my heart broke.

Although there really wasn't anything wrong with what my son said, the reality of what he was facing made me a little sad. Rather than say something nasty, or place blame on my ex, I told my son, *"Your Daddy will always be a part of our family. We are all family together and you are so lucky that so many people love you."* We then started naming all of the family members (both on my side and also his father's).

I felt, at that point, that it was so important to be inclusive, to normalize the situation, and to make my son feel encouraged to talk about all his family members, despite which parent he was living with at the time. Irrespective of how our relationship ended and why our marriage broke down, I have an ongoing obligation to my son to protect him from the hurt and the pain. I am responsible to give him the best possible experience of divorce so that when he grows older he looks up to me and feels proud of what I did for him.

As part of the Harmony Week celebrations that I spoke about above, my son's pre-school also required the children to dress up reflecting their culture and family background. I immediately thought to dress him in an Italian football jersey to reflect my Italian heritage, but I then paused to think about whether this was putting my son in a position of conflict. He has both Italian and Greek heritage (his dad being of a Greek background). Was it my responsibility to dress him in something that was a bit of both Italian and Greek? Or should I at least give my ex a nudge to dress him in something Greek later in the week when my son was in his care?

The conflict I battled came from something that had started as a humorous joke at home, but that I soon realized was actually causing my son distress in his little head. You see, we have weekly dinner at my parents' home each Tuesday. After I collect my son from pre-school, we drive over to my parents' place and usually enjoy some pasta and a little red wine (if we are lucky). Dad will often joke about being *Italiani* and say things to my son like, *"You have big muscles because you are an Italiano boy,"* or, *"You are so smart because you are Italiano like Nonno."*

Now, we know it is all joking around and a little fun, but for my son, it became a little debate. He would come back with *"No, Nonno, I'm Greco,"* or, *"My muscles are big because I am a Greek boy."* We all knew it meant nothing whether he was Italian, Greek, or Australian. But it was funny, and we continued. That was, until my son started saying, *"Nonno, can my cousin (who is Greek) come to your house on the weekend? I promise he will be Italiano when he comes over."*

From that moment, we know the joke had probably gotten out of hand and we had inadvertently caused him to feel like he had to pick sides or couldn't speak about paternal, other family with us. As adults, we often forget that it's the little messages we send kids that matter the most.

That one, almost insignificant moment during Tuesday family dinner night, was my wake up call to realizing how important it was to practice was I preached. I had to be extra careful with what I said about my son's dad, both to him and in front of him to other people. This was, above almost all else, so incredibly important.

Above all else, a child's experience of divorce stems from the messages sent by their parents via actions and words. Children are not, and should not be, responsible for their parents' emotions.

Children should not be made to feel caught between two competing homes. The best thing we can do as parents is to shield our children from the turbulence that comes with separation and divorce. That is the best way we can safeguard their emotional wellbeing and heal their wounds. It is through the words we speak and the behavior that we model that we really do protect our children and encourage them to have a healthier development. Easy to say, though, right?

> *"Parents are the ultimate role models for children. Every word, movement, and action has an effect. No other person or outside force has a greater influence on a child than the parent."*
>
> **—Bob Keeshan**

It is a normal thing to talk to your child about their other parent. In fact, it's good for your child to hear you speak about and engage in positive conversation about your co-parent. It is also normal to be inquisitive about stepparents or siblings. It is common to feel inclined to wonder about your child's other home, their other bedroom, and how they spend their time when not with you. It'd be odd not to wonder, at times, what your child's other life is like. How does he/she feel during the days apart from you? Do they fall asleep easily in their new bed? Do they tell bedtime stories? How involved is their stepparent? Again, normal things to ponder about.

I know that when my child returns from time with his dad, I always ask, *"How was your weekend with dad? What did you get up to and who did you see?"*

Rather than cross-examining my son about these topics, however, I keep our conversation focused on him. I only ask what needs to be asked for the purpose of having some healthy conversation and to encourage my child to feel normal and comfortable telling me about his time with his dad and the other people in his life. I think it is important for children to feel comfortable talking to each parent about the other.

The last thing I want for my son is for him to come home on a Sunday evening and feel unable to tell me about his day at the beach or the lunch he had with his dad and paternal family. Although we might not want to hear about our ex's life, it is still something special for our child. We want our children to be able to express themselves without fear of retribution for being happy and loving both their parents.

We promote unhealthy development in our children when we cause them to feel guilty about speaking about their other parent. There should never be a time when our child feels fear in telling us about their other parent. Once a child starts to change the dynamic of their conversation in order to protect a parent's emotions, things need to change.

If we find ourselves, as parents, falling into the trap of guilt-trapping our child about what their other parent has done or criticizing the way their other parent may have handled a situation, we need to stop and reflect on our own behavior. What does this reflection look like? If you can't have healthy conversation about what your child did with their other parent, don't ask.

Do not criticize your co-parent's choice of activity for the day. Do not question or cross-examine your child about their other parent's skills (for example, whether they put sunscreen on, whether they made your child wear a hat, whether they allowed your child to sit on their Play Station all day, or whether they fed your child fast food). You don't need to know every detail.

Keep conversation child focused. If your child mentioned they went to the movies, comment about what an exciting experience that would have been. Talk about popcorn, movie characters, and storyline. It is less important who else was there, whether the snacks provided were junk food, and whether the movie was inappropriate. Those types of comments can be raised with their co-parent away from your child (if necessary).

Encourage your child to bring toys or gifts between homes if they want to. Children of separation often struggle with fear of retribution for being given gifts by their other parent or a stepparent. They fear bringing the gift to their other home. Even if you feel that your co-parent is buying your child's love, this isn't something your child needs to know. Show excitement about the gift. Allow your child to express their happiness and let your child know it's okay to bring the gift home and then bring it back next time.

Do not make your child feel uncomfortable sharing news with their other parent. Do not cause your child to feel guilt or fear about which parent they share news with first. Encourage excitement about changeovers and be happy to speak about your child going off to their other parent. Many children of separation dread changeover day and feel guilty for hurting their parent, who might be saddened by their child leaving.

Normalize talking about previous family memories. It is okay to look at old photos and talk about your pregnancy, early birthday celebrations, or even family holidays. Your child wants to know about happier times. Don't complain about money, child support, or how hard it is to be a single parent.

Healthy Dinner Table Discussions

Imagine it is Friday night and you are about to sit down with your children and have dinner. You have made your daughter's favorite pasta bake and your son's favorite lemon cake for dessert. It is a no television, no device dinner. What sorts of things are healthy dinner table discussions, particularly with respect to their other parent?

Encourage chatter around fun activities your child can do with their other parent. This might include a day out or following a new recipe if your child likes baking. Talk about achievements at school or in sports and encourage your child to share this news with their other parent.

It is okay to be excited (or feign excitement if need be) about something exciting in your child's other parent's life. This might be a family wedding, upcoming holiday, or a home renovation.

Never throw your co-parent under the bus and don't play the blame game. Even if your co-parent won't, for example, let you take your children ice skating on the weekend, do not say to your children, *"I wanted to take you ice-skating but you mom/dad won't let me."*

It's okay to talk generally about finances. For example, *"Going to Hawaii is a little expensive at the moment. Why don't we look at going away for the weekend to the local beach?"* You should never throw your co-parent under the bus by talking about child support or saying things such as, *"If your mom/dad really loved you they would pay for your tickets to Hawaii."* Remind your children they are loved by both parents. A child can never experience too much love.

Many parents think that the more transparent they are with the children, the better. Truth is, less is more. Just because it happened, or just because you think it, doesn't mean your children need to hear it. Irrespective of their age, or how mature you think your children are, there is absolutely no truth in thinking your child needs to hear about how bad or unfair their other parent is.

Sure, your ex might be the biggest terror on the planet. He/she might still be toxic in their communication toward you. They might be the reason you can't afford your rent or mortgage this month. It is probably because of them that your child isn't going to the summer camp they are dying to go to next month with their friends. Even so, speaking kindly, or saying nothing at all, is far better than telling the truth. This is for your child's sake. Think about what you are going to say before you say it and think about what long-term impact will be had on your child because of what you are about to say.

I agree, in the short term, it probably feels better telling your kid how awful their other parent has been this week. You feel better telling your child you aren't the reason they are missing out on the activity they are so eager to do. You so badly want to be the parent they look up to, adore, and tell their friends about. And you want your child to know how terrible their other parent has been.

The reality is, despite your relationship having fallen apart, unless one of you has harmed your children, the relationship between child and parent will continue to be as important as ever. Despite your anger, resentment, sadness, and guilt, the relationship between child and parent needs to be protected. It is a lifelong relationship that only you have the power to maintain, safeguard, and encourage. Do so, even when it causes you heart ache.

I spoke earlier about my client, Samantha. She is the one in an extremely high conflict, post-separation relationship. I remember a Friday at the office when I received an email from her ex-husband's lawyers. The email had a link to a folder of dozens of recordings her ex-husband had taken of her. The recordings showed both parents in constant screaming matches. There is little doubt that the recordings themselves were wrong, illegal even.

My immediate concern, however, was the contents I was actually listening to. Parents berating one another for their faults, mistakes, and personal issues, but doing this in the presence of their two young children—and even worse, involving those children. I heard things like, *"Your dad called me a __."* *"Did you see that? Your dad just pushed me."* *"Your mom is taking all my money. She is going to cause us to lose our home."*

These two parents were so caught up in their hate and anger toward one another that they thought the best thing to do was to involve their kids, try to get them on side, and "win." In reality, they were sending the worst kind of message you can to a kid. They were crushing their little boys' worlds, telling them their other parent was the worse person on earth. They were encouraging their children to blame their other parent for the disrupted living environment they were experiencing, for the pain, and for the hurt.

Trust me, children do not need to know these things. They do not need to be involved in the heartache, pain, blame, hurt, or the conflict. Pick up your journal or start writing an email to yourself. Write about everything that is bothering you. Write your truth. Let out your emotions. Tell your journal how awful your co-parent is being and how unfair it is that they can't see eye to eye with you on this issue. Go into detail about how much this is affecting you and how badly you want your child to know the truth about what is going on.

Now, put your journal away in a locked drawer. Save your email into a private folder on your server. Look ahead and think about something positive. You are blessed. Yes, life can be hard at times. Things one hundred percent aren't fair, and you are in a position you probably don't want to be in. But you have made the decision today not to involve your child in ongoing conflict.

You have protected your child from the burden of choosing between parents and the burden of protecting your emotions. You stopped to pause and reflect on what your child really needed to know and you put your child first. Good job—truly. This is what being a collaborative co-parent is all about.

If we put things into perspective, it is important to remember that your child was created (literally) by you and your ex. The DNA within your child is a mix of you and their other parent. The good, the bad, the fun, the betrayal, every tiny little part within them is made up of both their parents. This is important to remember when you are about to tell your child something about their other parent.

By telling your child, *"Your dad is a liar. He hurt me,"* or, *"Your mom is an evil witch. She nags and complains all the time,"* your child is effectively being told that a part of them is not good. If their mom or dad is evil or a liar, are they also bad? Are you unintentionally telling your child that biologically they are just as a bad as their other parent? If they are just as bad as their other parent, how will this affect their self-esteem into the future?

Having said that, there are times when you should speak with your child neutrally about red flags concerning your ex. Saying this such as, *"It's never okay for someone to yell and call you rude names,"* or, *"No one should be hitting you or hurting you. That is not okay"* is, in my view, appropriate.

Talking about healthy behaviors without directly mentioning your co-parent allows you to guide your child and let them know what is okay, without blaming or causing them to feel guilty about their other parent.

My client, Amanda, came out of a long marriage with a history of abuse and trauma largely influenced by her ex-husband's untreated mental health issues. Despite this (and with years of effective therapy) she still acknowledged the importance of not involving her children in the conflict and the anger. Instead, she chose to protect her children via her communication with them about their dad.

> *"When the milk is splattered all over the floor, and those little eyes are looking at you for your reaction, remember what really matters. It takes five minutes to clean up spilled milk; it takes much longer to clean up a broken spirit."*
>
> **—Rebecca Eanes**

Rather than endlessly recount stories of the abuse to her children or repeat how bad and volatile their father had been, she prepared them for the time they were to spend with him. She talked to them about safety measures, warning signs, and things to do if they felt uneasy or unprotected. She didn't direct this to being about their father necessarily, but managed discussions around ensuring they had the right education about speaking up and feeling safe.

Often, her children did bring up incidents they remembered, including a time when Amanda and her ex-husband were in a deep argument about her working too much and him being responsible for washing up and packing away toys.

Her son recounted a memory of his father grabbing a bowl of porridge and pouring it over Amanda's head and then throwing a toy car directly at her face, causing blood to come gushing down her forehead. There is absolutely no excuse for that sort of behavior. I don't even suggest that such a violent relationship would at all warrant any type of co-parenting relationship. Safety will always come first.

For Amanda though, she did not want her children growing up feeling blame or guilt for these memories. Her son was already suggesting it was his fault for not having finished his breakfast or packing away his toys, causing his dad to become violent toward his mother. This is the perfect example of children developing memories and feelings based on what they see and hear.

Amanda repeatedly explained to her children that their father was unwell, and that he needed help and guidance in managing his emotions. She made sure to constantly remind her children that none of what they experienced was their fault, and in turn, likely not their father's fault either.

Did she need to do that? Probably not. Would she have wanted to tell her children what a bad man their dad was, that he caused her years of hurt, anger, and fright? I am sure. Did she want to tell them that she still walked down the street, scared that he might approach her? Sure. Deep down, did she want the world to know that she was struggling and it would take years of further therapy just to manage the emotions she continued to feel? I have little doubt.

Her top priority, however, was protecting those two children from being further impacted by their history. The prime message she wanted to send to them was that they were safe, they were not to blame, that mental health is a bigger issue than they understood, and that she was there to protect them. For Amanda, blame was not a priority. Her priority was her children's development and their mental health.

"The best, most mature co-parents will tell their therapist—and not their child—how much the other parent sucks."

—**Hayley Gallagher**

The messages we send, however, don't just come from what we say and the words we use. Our children are like sponges—big, beautiful, soft, and malleable sponges. Every little thing we do they observe, take in, and often, mimic. This counts for both the good things we do and the bad. I have a bad habit of using my hands way too expressively when I speak, and more so when I am angered.

I will literally be driving in traffic and if someone cuts me off, I shake my hands in the air. It's a bad habit, and it's one that my son has picked up on. If he gets cranky, he will often shake his little hands in the air, trying to be just like me. Perhaps he thinks it will have some positive effect in getting what he wants? He will convince me by shaking his hands aggressively in the air and pointing his little index finger. Truth is, I just laugh internally and tell myself I really need to do better. This extends to how I react and engage with his dad.

There are times no parent wants to interact with their co-parent, particularly if you have been cheated on, betrayed, or gone through a really difficult break up. It might just be that you are having a rather bad day at work, a fight with your new partner, or been given same bad news about your friend. You're not eager to have to put on a brave face and chat with your ex at changeover. Life would be so much easier if your child could just get out of the car and walk down the driveway and into the house. The reality however, is that many parents still do face-to-face changeovers and interact with their co-parent on special occasions (such as school assemblies or other important events for the child's sake).

If I rolled my eyes every time my son's father said something that got under my skin or raised my tone of voice and pointed my index finger in his face every time we disagreed, how would that make my son feel? I might say the right things at home, *"Your daddy loves you, he is a great person, and you are so lucky to have him,"* but if I send the opposite message with my actions, what impact is that going to have on my son?

Even still, if I am nice to his father at changeovers, engage in chitchat, smile, and am pleasant, but when I get together with my sister or my friends and my son is present and I bad mouth his father, cry about what he has done, or my body language changes when he is brought up, isn't this just as bad as speaking ill of him directly to my son?

The very powerful reality in the dynamic between a child and their parent is that no matter what we say, it is our actions that convey the strongest message. Despite what we may think, our children always pick up our emotional energy and behaviors. I could say the loveliest thing to my son about his dad, but if I have teary eyes

> *"If your actions don't live up to your words, you have nothing to say."*
>
> —DaShanne Stokes

and I'm shaken up, my son knows there is more going on than what I am saying. Irrespective of how old he is, my son knows when something is wrong with me.

If I look down, my energy is flat, or the tone in my voice is raised, he will often ask, *"What's wrong mamma?"* I think it is because of his childhood innocence that he won't know what is happening, but truth is, it is that very childlike curiosity that makes children more susceptible to knowing what is going on. Children by nature are more sensitive to our behaviors. It is our actions and behaviors that will indeed have the biggest impact on our children as they venture into teenagers and then adulthood. I can assure you that my son will remember the way I raised my voice or shook my hands in a much deeper way than he will remember the specific things I said.

I think that it is even harder for a child to navigate the world when they experience an inconsistency between words and actions. Why is their parent saying one thing, but acting so differently? Why does dad say he loves mom and she is a good parent, but then gets angry when she calls us? Why does dad mock mom with his friends, but is polite to her when he drops me off to her house? Children are curious. Children want to know the why's and how's.

Even if we don't tell them, they lie in bed at night and muster up ideas to support the how any why. They try to understand the conflict between their parents' behaviors and the words they speak. This is why it is so important for us as parents to be cognizant of the things we do and how it affects our children.

This also goes for the things we tell our family members and friends about our ex. Gossip feels good. It passes the time. A wine with a girlfriend, together with an antipasto board of cheeses, dips, and deli meats, is nice. So is girl chat while the kids sit near us playing on their devices or watching a movie. Little ears, however, are always listening. It is for this very reason that we need to set boundaries with our friends and family.

Setting Boundaries Amongst Friends and Family

Know it is not okay to start talking about your ex with your children around. Stop others from raising or denigrating your ex—it's not chatter that needs to be had around children. If you really need to vent, wait until the kids are in bed at night and save it for a late-night phone call or girls lunch without the children.

It's normal for your friends, siblings, and parents to want to be on your side, advocate for you, and tell you how crappy your ex is. They often feel like they are doing the right thing by being on your side, but what they are really doing is sending the wrong message to your child.

So, if we feel ourselves becoming angry, upset, or in the early stages of the need to vent, what can we do to avoid inadvertently involving our children?

Leave the room. Go for a walk or take a shower. Meditate. Close your eyes and count to ten. Take five slow, deep breaths. Put on some uplifting music. Take yourself away to read your book. Call a friend and organize a play date for your child if you're feeling vulnerable, or at a breaking point. Give yourself some time out.

Arrange an appointment with your therapist. It's okay to seek help. A psychologist or counselor is there to make navigating this stressful time easier.

Doing It for The Kids: Why Positive Communication About the Other Parent Is Paramount

Speaking of messages, when we talk about being a collaborative co-parent, and the impact of the messages we send our children, that extends to the way we use our children as messengers, as innocent as it might seem. Parents often don't recognize the impact even the most innocent of conversations have on children.

Many separated parents will have their children tell their other parent things like, "Dad said he will collect us at 4 p.m. today," "Mom wants us to give you these forms to complete," or, "Dad said he won't use the sunscreen you recommended. He has his own." What parents fail to see is that any negative response or reaction from the other parent will immediately impact a child and cause them to feel blame or guilt and is likely to cause unnecessary anxiety and distress.

When parents use their children to send messages and to communicate, children learn to ignore and substitute their own emotional and developmental requirements. They become mouthpieces for their parents and above all else, become advocates for a sense of fairness.

Using a child as a messenger during divorce instantly creates a role-reversal between parent and child. The child becomes protective of the parent. They take responsibility of their parent's emotions and stress about being the peace keepers in the family.

Kids know their parents can't communicate and can't agree on anything, so they really do push away their own feelings and needs to cater to the needs of their parents.

This can become emotionally exhausting for children the longer it goes on. Children stop enjoying their childhood. They experience resentment, confusion, and start to dread being placed in the middle of their parents' conflict. They also often start experiencing insecurity about their role within their family.

As parents, we are supposed to protect our children from emotional trauma. It is our role to make decisions for our children to lessen the burden on their little brains. Yet, for some reason, during separation, we often (intentionally or not) prioritize our own emotional health and avoid discussing the tougher issues with our other parent. We rely on our children to relay messages between households instead.

Or, it might be that we have such a dislike for our co-parent, that we (almost immaturely) think it will hurt them to use our children as messengers to send a clear message that our co-parent is no longer deserving of communicating directly with us. We do this, forget about the emotional burden we place on our children, and forget the long-term impact this will cause them. Social science tells us that the greater the emotional pressure and burden on children to please and protect a parent, the greater the devastating long-term impact on that child in future adult relationships, ability to have intimacy, and even ability to regulate adult emotions.

My friend, Jemma, had two young girls with her now ex-partner. She was sitting at home one night and he had left his iPad at home. Messages between him and a lover started coming through and she slowly learned about his years of infidelity. Trust between them was destroyed. Needless to say, they had a really poor co-parenting relationship at the start.

She was devastated. Her entire life was thrown upside down and she had a five and seven-year-old to look after, almost solely. He initially showed little interest in being involved in his daughters' lives and prioritized his new freedom, partying, drinking, and holidaying regularly. This only caused more pain for Jemma and her ability to communicate with him was destroyed.

Jemma refused to talk to her ex and insisted on her daughters relaying him messages. This would include instructions about their schooling and homework, when they needed medications, and eventually turned into her daughter's relaying to their dad the impact his behavior was having on their mother, the financial disarray they were experiencing, and the blame she placed on him.

Jemma soon learned that her daughters were withholding his nasty responses, and instead, navigating the emotion behind their parents' conflict by creating their own fake responses to protect her from more pain. Both girls were suffering emotionally. It was not until the elder child started displaying quite significant signs of deteriorating mental health and suicidal ideation that Jemma woke up to the difficult reality that both she and her ex-husband needed to shape up, communicate better, and stop involving their children in their communication and conflict.

When it comes to the point that you feel unable to directly communicate with you co-parent, redirect your hurt and anger to consider the potential negative impact that involving your children in the communication process may have. Find alternate ways to communicate that protects you from feeling too vulnerable, hurt, or angry. This might include:

- Using an application, as we discussed above.
- Using a dedicated email address that you only check at certain times.

- Maintaining a communication book with your ex.
- Engaging with a third party for communication, such as a parenting coordinator, conflict coach, or family therapist.
- Having pre-organized time for discussions away from children or new partners.

CHAPTER 6:

Accepting and Coping with the Impact of Separation on Children

Learn the Warning Signs, Navigate Emotions, and Heal Trauma and Emotional Dysregulation

Social science tells us that even as adults, children of divorce struggle with understanding and contextualizing their parents' separation. The way they see the world, behave in adult relationships, and respond to even their own children, is shaped largely by their experience of their parents' separation, despite how old they were when it happened.

Most young children remember seeing one of their parents leaving the family home. They can remember the yelling, the fights, and the tears rolling down one or both their parents' faces. Young children often don't know why their parents separated and cannot understand what is happening. This leads them to constantly question what went wrong, wonder if they were to blame, and try to figure out what could have happened differently. Teenagers feel anger, often become caught between both parents' emotions, feel guilt, blame, and then act out.

Parents who separate unknowingly involve their children in the conflict of divorce by exposing them to the ups and downs of the relationship breakdown and the roller coaster of emotions. Children are not able to make sense of what is happening or why emotions are being felt by one of their parents. The exposure to these feelings and dynamics of the relationship breakdown, however, can cause children to feel responsible for their parents' emotions. Children will attempt to manage the situation by controlling the emotions their parents experience. They will often mask their own feelings to lessen their parents' burdens.

The experience of divorce can also lead children to more strongly fear abandonment and loss. The more they are exposed to conflict, the more children struggle to understand that conflict. The notion that conflict leads to separation and possible abandonment becomes a constant source of struggle in a child's mind and can transcend into adulthood. Many of these feelings are normal. Children go from living in one home with stability to experiencing a life-changing shift to their constant.

I think that it is fair to say that not all children cope with divorce in the same way and not all children will be impacted identically. Each individual response will be shaped by a child's involvement and experience of their parents' separation. There is little doubt that ongoing parental conflict

"Let your hopes, not your hurts, shape your future."
—**Robert H. Schuller**

and poor behavior following a separation will cause a child to be impacted more significantly.

Isn't this the exact reason why we need to put our children first and become more collaborative co-parents?

Coping with Solo-Parent Life

As I have said earlier in this book, separation is tough. Those first few days and months bring up so many challenges. You are learning to cope with a new reality and a life you may never have imagined for yourself. All of a sudden you find yourself juggling the morning routine solo. You are scrambling for school socks, clean uniforms, brushing teeth, doing hair, making breakfast and school lunches, and rushing out of the house solo. You are managing school pick-ups, which might even involve several daycares, schools, and extra-curricular activities. You are the only one home to help with homework, get dinner ready, and put the next load of washing on.

Not to mention, you must hang the clean clothes, fold them once dry, and sort. You are the one organizing school bags for the following day, cleaning the dirty plates, storing the leftovers, and doing the bed-time routine. That might involve baths, teeth, pajamas, and stories, or monitoring use of technology in the bedrooms. Whatever your circumstances, you are coping with solo-parent life . . . and it certainly isn't easy.

I remember being at home with my one-year-old when I separated and thinking, *"How am I going to get everything done now?"* We tend to become reliant on the other parent helping us get through the day-to-day. I panicked at the thought of when my next shower would be, how I would wash my hair, and where I would leave this little being while I did the things I could so easily do before my separation.

The panic slowly goes away, and a routine slowly forms. I learned to shower only once he was asleep and dry my hair while he watched an episode of *Bluey* or *Peppa Pig*. I slowly gained the confidence to go to the local coffee shop solo, enjoy a babycino and some banana bread with my son, and enjoy Friday dinner dates just the two of us. We found our new normal, and that was okay.

Don't Involve the Children: When Parents Are Too Dependent on Their Children

Post separation, many parents find solace in their children. They replace the relationship they had with their ex-partner or spouse with their child. Sometimes this might just be in the form of doing dinner dates or move nights together. For others, it's finding a new gym buddy or training partner. For some parents, however, the new normal becomes late night chats and deep and meaningful conversations with their children.

We miss the warmth and comfort of having someone in our bed at night, so we start having our children lie in bed with us each night. We miss having someone to sit down at dinner time with and gossip, so we start sharing our problems with our children. We tell them about the issues with people at work, the frustration we have with our unsupportive families, or worse, we starting telling them about how bad their other parent is.

What we don't realize is that this often means placing an unintentional emotional burden on your child. We place a reliance on our children for emotional stability and support. They become the new constant for us. We do our shopping, coffee runs, and Saturday night dinners out with our kids. But is the normal? Is this healthy? What impact can this have on our children?

Rather than our children becoming our security blanket and our source of reassurance, we need to remember that it is our children who need safety, security, and stability from us. Does our ability to be there for our children diminish, though, for a period following our divorce?

When we are going through an emotional earthquake of our own, do we forget to check in and give our children the time they deserve? Do we replace their need for comfort with a need to fill the gap we are experiencing? The reality is that although our children may be hurting, we often downplay that pain to stop ourselves from feeling more guilt and anxiety.

I remember a client, Sarah, who once told me about the closeness of her relationship with her daughter following separation. Her daughter was about thirteen-years-old. They did their nails together fortnightly and went on coffee and dinner dates. They shopped together each weekend, sat down to gossip over a wine/juice, and lied in bed at night chatting about everything. It all seemed cute and innocent at the beginning. But the more I got to know my client, the more concerned I grew.

Sarah had become unable to make a single decision without running it past her thirteen-year-old daughter. This included things about their divorce proceedings, men Sarah had met online on Bumble, financial decisions, health issues, everything. Her daughter had become her constant emotional support in place of her husband. But, was that healthy for either of them?

How would her daughter feel knowing how much stress and grief her dad was causing her mom? Sarah would tell her daughter each time she got a nasty text from her dad, each time we received a cranky legal letter, and would ask her about her views as to next steps in both their property settlement and custody matter. She would bring her to appointments despite my requests for her not to have her daughter at meetings. In Sarah's head, how could she not? Her daughter was her everything. According to Sarah, each decision was "their decision."

I would often observe Sarah's daughter to be quiet, a little withdrawn, and cautious. The reliance upon each other was obvious, even in a physical sense. Social science tells us that parents in significant emotional distress often cannot identify when their child is suffering. They may not immediately realize that their child is uncomfortable in a situation or feels overwhelmed and anxious. The reality of such a codependent attachment is that a parent like Sarah probably didn't realize the impact her relationship with her daughter was having on her daughter.

Her daughter needed reassurance, guidance, and even authority. She didn't need a close, dependent friendship with her mother. Separation is a lonely and daunting time for children, and becoming their parents' emotional support can make the experience even more daunting and create ongoing security and confusion.

As a family lawyer, I constantly tell my clients not to go home and involve their children in adult decisions. I urge them not to tell their children that their other parent won't let them go on the overseas holiday that's coming up, or that their other parent stopped paying maintenance this month.

A golden rule of divorce is not to place the emotional burden of parental conflict on your child.

As adults, we often forget that our children are incapable of emotionally dealing with separation. They are not equipped to really understand the ins and outs of the decisions being made or the emotions experienced by the parents.

I always say that what happens within our home plays the biggest part in shaping our child's experience of divorce or separation. As a mom, my perspective remains the same, but my practical experience is obviously a little different. I am not going to lie and say that it has always been bells and whistles for my co-parent and me. We didn't fall into a place of co-parenting bliss straight after our separation. And I won't lie, there have been many nights

I wanted a cuddle buddy to sleep with, so I let my three-year-old creep into the covers and cuddle all night long.

There are days I become incredibly cranky with my co-parent and I know my child is in the room listening. There has been the occasional eye roll or two over Facetime when I hear my co-parent say something to my son. I definitely am not perfect. I live in the same reality as you. I do however, recognize when the behavior I am displaying is bad for my child.

I don't want my son to end up struggling with how to act in an adult relationship, trying his best not to be like his parents. It is perfectly normal to cry yourself to sleep some nights, to feel insecure, to become angry at your co-parent, and to crave someone to open up to each night. It's okay to spend more time than usual with your child, and it's even okay for your child to become your new best friend. What's not okay is unloading the emotional burden of divorce or separation on your child, and forcing an interdependent attachment upon them.

Regressive and Anti-Social Behavior by Children

We often focus so closely on what we are losing by the end of a relationship or marriage, that we seem to ignore the really big losses our children experience with the end of their parents' relationship. We have a responsibility to be at the forefront of helping our children to recognize and cope with these losses and changes.

With separation and divorce brings really big, life-changing grief for children. How they then cope with that grief comes down to how we guide our children and the environment we build for them. There are everyday changes that our children experience that we often forget about and minimize. These include:

- Losing their family home, either all together, or for half the time.
- Familiar surroundings: neighbors, school friends, practitioner, and people children became used to seeing most days and who might not be around if a change of home or neighborhood is necessary.
- Seeing one of their parents daily: Children go from seeing both parents every day to going days or even weeks without seeing one parent.
- A change to their routine: Children may have had a stay-at-home mom or dad who now has to work post separation. Children are now going to after-school care, being looked after by a grandparent or nanny, and experiencing a shift to what they know.
- Extended family members who they may not see as often when they are going between homes.
- The need to explain their home situation to classmates, teachers and friends, and the shame or embarrassment that may come with that.
- The pressure of deciding which parent to tell first about an achievement.

We forget that our children didn't get a choice in their parents' separation or divorce. They were thrown into a life-changing experience with no say and often no warning. I agree wholeheartedly that a separation can be better for children in circumstances of significant parental conflict and a toxic home environment. This doesn't, however, make it any easier.

Just as we take time to grieve the loss of our life partner, children need time to grieve and accept the change to their family dynamic, which might include the loss of one primary parent.

This period of grief requires an understanding by parents and recognition of the need for comfort, reassurance, support, and above all else, love.

Children need time to understand, reflect, bargain, feel angry, feel sad, accept, and move forward. This does not happen overnight. The movement through the reflection, angry, sad, and bargaining stages to a sense of acceptance and ability to see the positive in their new life is only possible with the support of their parents. Both parents.

This is where the collaborative co-parent style of separated parenting comes in. Despite the anger we may feel toward our co-parent, the differences in opinions, morals, or the hurt we feel, our children need us to show up and work with our co-parent to guide our children through their grief. Even for younger children, this need for support is so important.

Just because a child is not old enough to voice their sadness and anger about their parents' separation does not mean that they don't experience the same train ride of emotions to acceptance. Younger children immediately feel the loss of a parent within their home. They soon realize that one parent is not around as often to give them a bath at night, to read the nighttime story, or to go for family walks on a weekend.

They observe and experience the loss of seeing their parents working together within the home. They will struggle with the new sense of routine. But with guidance, emotional support, reassurance, and love, they will find comfort and stability in their new sense of home.

My son was only one when my co-parent and I separated. He went from living a life with two parents who were around for mealtimes, rocking him to sleep, waking him up each morning, to one. His life had been seeing two smiles each time he reached a milestone, spending weekends with both his parents, going for walks, enjoying new cafés, and both of us taking him out for adventures.

Suddenly, that reality became moving out of a big home into two much smaller units and not seeing one of his parents for three to four days at a time. Don't get me wrong. He is an incredibly loved child with an abundance of affection, support, and laughter each day. Despite this though, he went through an incredibly life-changing experience at a young age.

All of a sudden, he was in an environment with two single parents coping with their new lives, understanding what separation meant, living in two new homes, and growing/changing/adapting at the same time. New milestones were met but observed and celebrated separately. Christmases, Easters, and birthdays were celebrated independently. Facetime became a new constant. The little blue backpack filled with toddler shoes, comforters, medicine, and nappy cream became a new permanent at each front door.

The changeover between his mom and dad became a big part of the week with so, so many tears at first, and overtime, less tears, and a deeper understanding that changeover just meant he would see one of us again in a few days' time. I immediately knew I had to implement important strategies and support my son through this adjustment and help him have a better experience of separation. What did this involve?

As hard as it was, it meant encouraging an equal time arrangement with my co-parent. This allowed for my son to become familiar and comfortable with both parents and both homes. My concern was always that if my son lived primarily with me and spent little time with his father, it would be harder and take longer for my son to adjust.

I spoke positively about my son's father to him each night. I would openly talk to my son about all of his family members. We would play games like, *"Who are we having birthday cake with this year?"* and we would list all our family members, both on my side and his dad's side. We did this not because we were going to have a joint birthday, but because I wanted my son know it was okay, acceptable, and safe for him to talk about all his family members, despite which parent he was with.

I made the lead up to changeover fun. I got my son excited to go to his dad. I shielded my son as best as I could from high conflict conversations. If I needed to vent to my sister or a girlfriend, I would have the call late at night when my son was in bed or when he was with his dad.

I encouraged card making and the buying of presents for days like Father's Day, birthdays, and Christmas. If I bought new dummies, comforters, or made a change to his routine, I let my co-parent know or bought doubles so that my son could have familiar items in both homes and follow the same routine as best as possible in both homes.

I purchased children's picture books about living in two homes. We read the books every night to normalize our new lifestyle.

We had lots and lots of cuddles. We had dinner dates, park dates, coffee dates, and enjoyed bike rides and ferry rides. I made the most of our days together.

My friend, Lucy, similarly experienced a separation when her daughter was only a few months old. She had a really different experience to me. Her relationship with her co-parent was high conflict. They disagreed about feeding, routine, co-sleeping, and involvement of other family members. Lucy's daughter resided full time with her and spent time with her dad once a fortnight at best, and not overnight until she was about three years old.

The separation took a huge emotional toll on her daughter, something Lucy did not recognize for years. Lucy's daughter suffered a significant regression at preschool. The emotional desire to mature did not eventuate as she placed all her focus on responding to the trauma of her parents' separation.

She was exposed to conflict, and it was obvious to her that her parents could not stand each other and were not on the same page when it came to her care. This also caused her to suffer significant separation anxiety from her mother. Changeovers were traumatic. She would be out of control, screaming and crying. She refused to leave Lucy. This then started happening at preschool, too. Lucy's daughter refused to sleep at her father's home. She did not eat, and she was constantly upset. This caused greater arguments between Lucy and her co-parent, who started disagreeing about routine, the need for greater stability, over attachment, co-sleeping, and what healthy parenting behaviors looked like.

Lucy soon realized the effect her poor co-parenting relationship was happening on her little one. Despite the intense conflict, she took it upon herself to introduce a healthier co-parenting relationship. She gave her ex tips to get their daughter to sleep. She packed snacks their daughter enjoyed and suggested activities. She slowly started allowing more overnight time and became more accepting of a routine in terms of their co-parenting arrangements. Lucy started speaking fondly of her ex around her daughter and formed a friendship with her ex's new partner to open a line of communication between the two homes.

Just because she could not communicate well with her ex didn't mean that her daughter had to suffer. She walked her daughter in to her father's home at changeover, rather than exchanging at the local park. This allowed her daughter to experience both parents being together, even for a short time. This encouraged feelings of safety, particularly in knowing Lucy was accepting of her being with her dad at his home.

These little changes made a huge difference in Lucy's daughter. Although there were still difficulties (and they still exchange the angry text or two), her daughter started to settle at changeovers, separated more easily at pre-school drop-off, and caught up to her peers emotionally and developmentally.

Sometimes we don't see how big a difference our behavior can have on the development of our children. Their sense of security and safety really does stem from how we interact with others around them and how we carry ourselves and behave in their presence.

"My mission in life is not merely to survive, but to thrive; and to do so with some passion, some compassion, some humor, and some style."

—Maya Angelou

A close family friend of mine, Nikki, took me for many coffee dates following my separation. She shared with me her experiences of coping with her children's emotional rollercoaster following her divorce. At the time she separated, Nikki's children were thirteen and fifteen-years-old. Undoubtedly, they were in the rough teenage years. She was faced with smashing doors, rebellious teenage behavior, loud music, risky activities, depression, and prolonged grief. Although she stayed in the family home with her girls, she almost thought this was worse. It took a long time for her girls to understand why their dad was not coming back, why he had moved into a unit in the next suburb and why they could only see him every second weekend.

In the early days, while recovering from her own separation trauma, she missed the warning signs. She didn't feel emotionally present enough to realize her children were suffering. She took the closed bedroom doors, the long late-night phone calls, and the absence of her children for the entirety of the weekend, as her children coping by spending time with their friends, on their iPad's, or watching Netflix. The reality was, her girls needed emotional support and didn't receive it early enough. They took to risky behavior and rebellious activities and became angry and depressed.

By eventually seeing the warning signs, Nikki took control of the situation. She urgently put in place a recovery strategy to help piece her family back together. Despite the terrible breakup she had with her ex-husband, she knew she needed to work together with him to get her daughters the right help. What did this come down to?

- Encouraging her daughters to spend more time with their dad rather than less.
- Being tougher with rules at home and ensuring her co-parent implemented the same rules in his home.
- Getting psychological help for her daughters and facilitating and encouraging their ongoing involvement with that support system.
- Talking, listening, being available for her daughters, and answering their questions.
- Getting the school involved as an additional support.
- Sheltering her daughters from legal proceedings, and any conflict with her ex.

As hard as it was, she also chose to be open and willing to listen to her daughters talk about their dad, have pictures of him around, share old memories, and encourage new memories.

Nikki also showed support by letting her daughters know it was okay to feel what they were feeling. Rather than condemn their poor behavior, she encouraged a way forward to acceptance.

Warning Signs and the Need to Be on the Same Page as Co-Parents

People often ask me, what are the warning signs? What do we look out for to know our children are not doing okay? This obviously changes depending on age and stages of development for a child. Not all children will experience a rollercoaster of emotions.

Some may adapt to change really well, and others may experience a flurry of every emotion under the sun and become a real challenge. Here are some of the observations made by the people I know and have spoken with when it comes to post separation parenting and warning signs:

- Wetting the bed after well-established toilet training.
- Refusal to sleep.
- Separation anxiety.
- Emotional regression.
- Developmental regression.
- Speech regression.
- Compulsive disorders. This could be over eating, under eating, cleaning, washing hands, or other actions to fill the void felt by the grief of parents' separation.
- Failure to share and being possessive of possessions.
- Lack of boundaries with friends and family members. Seeking comfort from others but having no boundaries.
- Risk taking behavior such as drugs, alcohol, smoking, and stealing.
- Failure to communicate with a parent and going out without notice of when they will be home.
- Changes in behavior at school.
- Learning difficulties.

Having said that, I don't have an answer or solution to stop each and every warning sign. It takes more than a quick fix, or a band aid to be placed over the issue. It comes down to stronger, more aligned co-parenting, support, reassurance, and often third-party intervention for most of the issues faced by children of separation or divorce. Sometimes it is the little things we do, however, that can influence a reaction in our children that encourages improvement or change. Here are some little everyday things we can do:

- Stop pressuring our children to pick sides.
- Encourage our children to care for both parents.
- Write little notes of love, self-care, and encouragement and pop them into our children's lunch boxes, clothes' pockets, and bed side tables.
- Surprise our children with their favorite meals when they least expect it.
- Encourage wholesome friendships with neighbors, school peers, and extended family members.
- Organize exciting and spontaneous adventures such as the movies, a skate park, rock climbing, or a weekend staycation at a nice hotel.
- Make an effort with your children when they least expect it. Take time out of work commitments to let you children know they are prioritized.

Importantly though, is the need for co-parents to communicate effectively and be transparent about their children's difficulties post separation. This is not an opportunity to place blame or increase conflict. There comes a time when a couple's differences really do need to be set aside and focus needs to be placed on how separated parents can work together to assist a child in need.

If this is impossible because of the level of conflict or safety/family violence issues, it is still recommended that you be transparent in the difficulties being experienced and propose steps for assistance and support. In situations of this nature, using a more appropriate communicate method might assist (email, a co-parenting application, or authorizing a support person including a therapist or general practitioner to speak with both parents).

Keep at the forefront of your mind how beneficial it is to a child to know that they don't have parents in conflict about what is best for them. Better still, think about how important it is for a child to know that they can't play parents off of each other and don't have one parent who will encourage risk-taking behavior and cover it up, and one strict parent who enforces the rules. Place importance on a child's need for parents to be united in times of challenge.

How can parents come together to show their children that although they are now living separately, their parents still love and support them and are united in their approach to the difficulties they are experiencing?

- Where possible, hold a family meeting. This can be at a neutral place. Allow your child to express anger or sadness.
- Emphasize that your child is not in trouble, you are not placing blame on them, and they are not at fault for the separation, divorce, or any ongoing conflict.
- Show support. Show love. Encourage open discussion.
- Reassure your child that they are important to both parents.
- Listen. Be open to suggestions made by your child.
- Make proposals for support.

- Do not speak over your co-parent.
- Do not go against your co-parent. Come up with a plan before the meeting.
- Stop yourself from using the common line when a child is misbehaving, "I am going to tell your mom/dad and they can deal with it."
- Be real. Give examples of when you have struggled, needed support, reached out for support, and felt better.

One of the hardest things to navigate following a separation with children, is how to maintain a sense of normalcy for your children. We are challenged by a desire to keep thing consistent and normal and to avoid change for our children. But how do we do this and also protect our own mental health and our own hearts?

Special Occasions, Functions, and Coming Together Jointly as a Separated Family

Special occasions are supposed to be a time of joy, togetherness, celebration, and family. For separated families, this idea of maintaining the normal and ensuring children don't miss out on those feelings of togetherness and family can create anxiety. It can also be a source of great stress and even conflict.

Everything from arranging parties and celebrations, to giving gifts, deciding on the inclusion of extended family, and co-parenting schedules can create challenges and make special occasions a dreaded time of year.

My son started pre-school this year. With this change came the weekly birth-

"When we deny our stories, they define us. When we own our stories, we get to write the ending."

—Brené Brown

day invitations to join his classmates and their families at birthday parties. When September came around and it was my son's turn to celebrate his birthday, I observed his confusion at why he was having two birthday parties. We had been doing this for years.

For his second birthday, I had a Madagascar themed party and his dad held a Disney party. For his third, we both had separate Spiderman birthdays. This year, it was *Paw Patrol* for me and Hot Wheels for his dad. On one hand, I think about how lucky my son is. Two parties, two cakes, two sets of presents and celebrations. At the same time though, I still get that little sinking feeling when I think about the loss he must feel when he goes between households to celebrate.

I see the reluctance he has to tell us each about the other's party: who was there, what he got, the excitement he felt. This was more so this year when I purchased him a toy electric guitar for his birthday, something he had been asking for over several months. We would sit in the car and sing to ACDC and other rock songs and he would exclaim how excited he was to be getting a guitar for his birthday.

Well, the birthday came around and he got not one, but two guitars. One from me, and one from his dad's partner. Obviously, his excitement and love of all things rock was being shared in both homes. Beautiful, I know. Did it hurt a little? Of course. Rather than be sour about the situation (and don't get me wrong, deep down I felt a little anger that she would get the same present as me), I wanted to show my son that he had every right to be excited and share that excitement with me and with his dad.

I encouraged him to tell me all the wonderful things about his birthday party with his dad. I shared in his joy and even asked his dad for photos of their special day so I could share these with my son, talk about them at night, and print them off for show-

and-tell at school. Our new normal wasn't going to be having one joint birthday party. Unfortunately, we still aren't there, and we may never be. But I still want my son to know he can always feel comfortable sharing things with both of us and be open, honest, and communicative with us about events and functions.

When we look at couples like Gwyneth Paltrow and Chris Martin, who seem to have mastered this notion of conscious uncoupling, it can often make us feel confused that we aren't able to come together as they can for their kids. Collaborative co-parenting, and indeed co-parenting itself, doesn't mean parents have to celebrate holidays or special occasions together.

Some families do really well at celebrating birthdays together. To avoid conflict, they set boundaries and put rules in place. Parents share tasks and assign jobs to avoid arguments. Mom might be in charge of the cake and decorations and dad might be in charge of drinks and being on barbeque duty. They forewarn family members who may not get along to sit separately and avoid contact, because conflict will only ruin a child's birthday.

I truly believe that we are doing better as a society today than in the past, and that with time, there will be more families living across two homes who maintain a close connection for their children. At the same time though, there will always be couples who won't be able to join together for celebrations or sit together at school or religious functions, and that is okay.

Often, it takes time to form that new relationship post separation. While the first months and even years are the toughest, this time can encourage co-parents to be okay with spending time together and with their children for functions and other events. It is likely that you won't be celebrating together in the beginning, but with time and healing, understanding and reflection, you might find yourself able to be together as your children get older.

New partners, stepsiblings and the craziness of life will come in the way, and everything you dreamed of has probably changed, but there is never a time limit on when you need to make final decisions on what you do with your co-parent for events.

Just because you couldn't sit together for primary school graduation doesn't mean that three years later, you can't join together for the end of middle school celebration. Even if you despise one another at your daughter's fifth birthday, you might be in a different place by the time her tenth birthday rolls around, where celebrating all together will come naturally.

Be open to change, and be open to allowing yourself the space to heal and make new decisions. Don't be afraid of judgment, don't listen to what your friends or extended family members have to say. Your parents might hate your ex because he cheated, but if celebrating a birthday or a school graduation together feels normal to you, do it. Be together. Put your child first and think about what would make them the happiest.

Just as we need to consider our own hearts, so too do we need to consider how celebrating together might impact our children. I think there is little doubt that where there is no conflict, children will always benefit from seeing their parents come together.

However, there is also social science which shows us that divorce has such a traumatic impact on children that in the early days, they need time to heal and adjust. Trying too hard to come together as a separated family for special occasions and holidays right after a divorce or separation can be confusing for children. The concept of being together can cause children to have false hope that their parents are reconciling and that the separation is not permanent. This in itself can interrupt the healing process.

Most people ask me, *"How do we know we are ready to join together for special occasions or functions?"* My advice is always:

communication is everything. I have said it before, and I will say it again. Have a clear line of open communication with your children about their feelings and where they are.

Some children will feel ready to be together with both their parents. However, if there has been significant conflict or even family violence, this may take longer, or never happen at all. Reassure your children. Listen. Be their earpiece and take on board their feelings.

Don't come together if you are faking you are okay with the situation. Pretending is the worst thing for children. Children are smarter than we think and will often pick up on when their parents are feigning interest in being together or holding it together just for them.

Self-care prior to an event is so important. What do you need to do to feel your best? Some might need the support and encouragement of a friend. Others may like to hit the gym before a stressful occasion. Do what is going to give you the most confidence and encouragement before an event for which you need a newfound courage.

Avoid events which have been a source of conflict in the past. If Christmas or Easter were occasions that caused upset or arguments during your marriage, those arguments are bound to linger, even following separation. The last thing your kids need is to see you and your ex making snarky remarks to the other about extended family members or complaining about which aunt or cousin will be at an event.

Avoid functions that will be tense and cause stress for your kids. Choose events that will promote harmony and allow your children to feel at ease. Remember, as the event comes around, your children will always feel a little pressure, even nervousness, at the thought of everyone being together. You don't want to cause more tension by arguing in their presence.

Don't tell your children your ex is joining an event unless you have confirmed this with them. The worst thing for a child is to get their hopes up and then feel that they are to blame when their other parent doesn't show up.

If you or your ex start to blur the boundaries of the separation and you start misinterpreting the joint family time as an opportunity to rekindle, put the brakes on. It might be that neither of you are ready for the time together and still need more time to heal. Opening up Pandora's box of memories and hurt can be detrimental to a person's ability to move past separation and divorce.

Start small. It's often easier to navigate jointly attending a basketball game or school ceremony than going to your ex-husband's family Christmas function. It might be that going to a classmate's birthday party together is easier, away from your own family and friends. To begin, pick the functions that you know will be easiest.

Keep rules in place. If having new partner attend a soccer match causes conflict, agree to leave those partners at home at first. Conflict needs to be avoided as much as possible for your children. The last thing a kid needs is to have their mom's new boyfriend at the soccer game yelling at their dad.

Chat about the right time to introduce new partners. At the same time, if sitting together at events is too much, agree to attend, but sit separately. If you decide you will all attend a religious or school function together, be clear about who is picking the outfit, the cake, buying the gift, and other details. Again, anything you can do to avoid conflict for your child needs to be at the forefront of your mind in every decision you make.

Be kind to yourself, to your children, and to your co-parent. Separation is stressful. It brings trauma, stress, and grief. You don't need to get it right on the first joint occasion. It might take three or four failed attempts at getting together before things fall together. Don't lose perspective of what's important, and don't mask the sadness you feel. Be kind and look forward. There is always going to be a next time and an opportunity to try again,

Extra Tips for The Holiday Season

As a family lawyer, by October of each year, I often deal with parents navigating the forthcoming holiday period. Who will have the children over for Christmas? How can the holidays be shared? What about our extended families? Can he/she come to the school Christmas concert?

My biggest piece of advice is for parents to try to work together and communicate about these issues early. Nobody wants to end up in court right before Christmas arguing about a time that is supposed to be happy. My tools and tips for the coming Christmas period?

Don't leave it until the last minute to agree on Christmas Day arrangements. What works well for some families is to alternate odd and even years (for example, from midday Christmas Eve until midday Christmas Day with one parent and from midday Christmas Day to midday Boxing Day with the other parent, alternating each year).

Keep negative discussions about your former partner or their family away from your child's hearing. The worst thing for children is to be involved in or within hearing distance of denigration about their other parent.

Consider agreeing to enough school holiday time with each parent to allow for the possibility of overseas or interstate travel. Be flexible and open minded. This is particularly relevant for children who have extended family internationally or across Australia.

Start a dialogue about present giving. It is always awkward when one parent buys an extravagant gift for their child. Try and set a joint budget, chat about your child's interests, and exchange ideas.

Talk about Santa. Have a collaborative view on how to explain what is happening to your child. Children who live in two homes may experience things differently but do not need to miss out on tradition.

Keep Christmas child focused. This is not a day for you or your ex. It is a day to ensure your children feel loved, supported, secure, and part of a healthy family environment.

Above all else, we need to remember that a strong, supportive, and focused relationship with our children is the most important part of assisting them to heal following a separation. Be sure to let your children know that they are not alone in the process. Everyone is hurting and everyone will be impacted differently. The anger you feel may not be the same anger your child feels.

> *"Letting go doesn't mean that you don't care about someone anymore. It's just realizing that the only person you really have control over is yourself."*
> **—Deborah Reber**

Irrespective of who is right or wrong in the situation, children need to feel reassured, safe, and secure in their new life. Most significantly, we need to remember that a relationship between parent and child is not equal in terms of the power dynamic. Parents need to be more powerful than children in that relationship.

We need to be able redirect emotions, provide security, and encourage regulation of emotions. Despite how hurt we feel, we need to prioritize being cognizant of the impact on our children and how our ability to manage the post separation process will shape our children's lives.

CHAPTER 7:
The Blended Family

The Brady Bunch: Fact or Faux?

The irony of sitting down to map out this chapter is that when I started this book, my life looked a lot different than what it does now. I started the concept for this book influenced by my work, together with my changing life situation. Fast forward to today and, although I continue to navigate the challenges of co-parenting and the ups and downs of raising a preschooler as a separated and divorced mom, I am now in a special new relationship with an incredibly supportive partner, with whom I'm expecting a baby any week. The juggle is real. The idea of the blended family is real.

I think I still wake up every day not knowing what to expect. I have a constant, internal conflict about how I'll watch my newborn grow and change daily, and yet I only get to do that for half the time with my son. I am navigating the challenges that come with making sure my two children aren't treated differently, don't feel different, and making sure I'm present for both of them. I am still navigating the challenges of being a co-parent. When did everything change and when did everything become more complicated? Or am I looking at it wrong, and rather than being complicated, is it special, unique, the new normal?

I always tell my clients that when they negotiate a parenting plan, particularly with young children, it is important to remember that what their life looks like now may be entirely different in two, three, or even five years' time. Clients always say to me, "*Oh, I am never marrying again*" or, "*I am so done having children.*" I will check in a few years later, and surprise , they have re-partnered or had another child. Life moves on and we grow and change.

The reality of separation is that one or both of you will likely re-partner and maybe even start a new family. That reality is a hard one. It comes with its own set of emotions, grief, acceptance, and understanding. You may have had a really tough separation, but knowing your previous partner has moved on and started a new family will bring a range of emotions. There is nothing wrong about feeling hurt or grieving a situation. Humans weren't created to be emotionless and mechanical in the way they perceive a situation. Our circumstances are all unique and we deserve time to reflect on a situation before moving forward.

> "*The blended family isn't just an ordinary family times two. It's a special kind of family with special needs.*"
>
> —**Maxine Marsolini**

When to Involve Children and How to Navigate Change

When we re-partner and have children in our lives, the imminent question is, "*When will I introduce my children to my new partner?*" For an ex, the imminent thought is likely, "*When is my ex going to introduce our kids to their new partner?*"

There is little doubt that the thought of your ex re-partnering will bring about a rollercoaster of feelings, good and bad. You might immediately put up your natural defensive mechanisms and feel a desire to protect or take control of the situation because they are "your kids" and why should "your kids" meet this new person? You may feel a rush of fleeting questions and concerns:

- Who is this person?
- What are they like?
- Will they replace me?
- Will my kids like this person more than me?

One of the hardest feelings will be knowing that your ex's partner will spend time with your children when you can't. The need to find the positive in this situation is what will make it easier for you, eventually. Your children will likely benefit from the time and experiences they make with this new person. As hard as it might be, trust that your ex does have your children's best interests at heart and will not introduce anyone unsafe or unsuitable to your children. Obviously, in the rare situation where there are safety issues, my advice does not apply and there are different matters you need to consider and seek advice on professionally.

Before introducing your children to a new partner, be cognizant of the fact that your ex may be sensitive about the situation. It has likely been a tough journey for you both to develop a good co-parenting relationship, and you don't want to change this. At the same time, you want to move on with your life and start a new future for yourself and your kids.

My view is that it is important to have a conversation with your ex, if possible, to establish basic guidelines around introduction of new partners that make you both comfortable and protect your co-parenting relationship. For some co-parents, having your ex and new partner meet before your children do might be preferable. This way, when you do start talking about your new partner and introduce your children, you can say that your mom or dad already know this new person and are happy for everyone to meet. This removes pressure from your children.

For other co-parents, you might work on introducing your children to your new partner, having told your ex of your plans, and once that relationship is established, you might have your new partner meet your ex. This is something I delve into below. I don't think there is any formula or best way of doing it. It really is about assessing your situation and dynamic and making a decision that will best promote stability and safety for your children and your family.

In terms of finding the right or best time to introduce a new partner to your children, I feel that it is always better to wait rather than rush into such a decision. Time is a good thing. Time allows you to be sure of your situation. Time allows your children to come to terms with their new dynamic. Speaking with your children about your new partner first also allows them to ask questions, understand, and even cope with the prospect of another change to their lives.

What should this communication look like? Is there a road map to how you should start the discussion and how involved your children should be? The answer is, not really. The primary focus should be on determining what discussion should be had based on your children's ages and maturity level.

So, for example, for little kids, you probably only need to go as far as telling them you have a new friend. Tell your child that this new friend makes you happy. Talk about things you can do together such as painting, playing with toy cars or barbies, and going to the park for ice cream. It is important you reassure your preschooler or young child that both their parents still love them and will continue to love them and look after them together. Encourage your young child's involvement in any plans for a meeting and make this special to your child.

For primary school children, you should still refer to your new partner as a new friend because stability is fundamental. You want to focus your conversation on your love for your child, that things won't change, and that you will still be around and prioritize your time with your child. Explain that your new friend would also like to get to know your child and spend some time together doing things you all enjoy. It is extremely important for school-aged children to know that they will continue to be supported by both their parents and that their other parent won't be affected by this further change.

For teenagers and older children, it is okay to explain that you are dating someone. It is important to reassure your teenager that you are in a committed relationship, that you both have the same values, and that it is important to you for your child to meet this person. You should still reassure your teen that you are there for them, that life won't be drastically changing, and that you are supportive of their feelings and how slowly or quickly they feel they want to be involved in your new relationship.

It is so important that you are sure of your new relationship before introducing your children to this new person. Is this person someone you see yourself spending your future with? Do you have the same values? Are on you the same page about rules, boundaries, and discipline of children? Have you spoken about how meeting your kids will look and how life will be once (and if) you move in together?

Having these conversations and being on the same page about important life matters is fundamental to the preservation of a solid new relationship. This safeguards your children from future attachment and then loss. Change is a big thing for kids. The last thing they need is to be introduced to partner after partner and feel a constant sense of loss or change. This can be significantly unsettling for children and impact them developmentally. Don't rush to introduce a new partner just to recreate the nuclear family you once had. Certainty is fundamental and your children's emotions need to be at the forefront of every decision.

As exciting as it might seem, children will still feel a sense of worry, need to protect their other parent, or just a sense of uncertainty about how a new partner will change their life with you. Will you have less time for them? Will this person come between you and them? Is there going to be another person setting rules and disciplining? Adjustment and time are key.

When the time does come, start slow and small. Keep the first meeting brief and think of doing something that will interest your kids and feel neutral. Some ideas include:

- Picnic and trip to the playground
- Lunch at a familiar local café or shopping center
- Swim at the local beach or lake
- Seeing a movie together
- Attending a local fair or circus

A neutral setting for a first meeting encourages children to feel more secure. Inviting your new partner into your home may cause your children to have their guards up. Remember that for kids, one of their biggest fears is having their other parent replaced. Reassure your children that your new partner is not going to replace their other parent or even step into that role. This new person is there to be a part of their lives in a way that your children feel comfortable with. Short bouts of time are always best at first.

It is also important that you spend one on one time with your children after a meeting to provide comfort, an opportunity to ask questions, help them feel heard, and to support them through another change in their lives. It is essential that your children know that all their time with you is not going to be spent only with this new person. They will still have time with you on their own. They still matter and they still come first.

Social science also tells us that children can, especially at the start of a new relationship, struggle with seeing too much physical affection. It is recommended that you limit physical displays of affection in front of your children. Having said that, offering an extra cuddle or kiss to your children in the presence of your new partner reassures your children that they have your unconditional love. Children who receive constant love and support from their parents generally develop greater emotional security in life and experience reduced anxiety.

Part of preserving that unconditional love is ensuring that you maintain routine and habits with your children. If Fridays have always been pizza and movie nights for you and the kids, don't stop. Keep the tradition going. It is important that your children know you still value that time together and that you prioritize it. As time goes on, and as your children become more familiar with your new partner, it might then be the right time to involve your partner in the tradition also.

The bottom line is that the involvement of any new partner in your children's lives will bring about all sorts of emotions, some arguments, and the need to navigate yet another big change. You are in control and responsible for

> "The sign of a great parent is not the behavior of the children. The sign of a truly great parent is the parent's behavior."
>
> —Andy Smithson

how your children are involved in the process. You need to recognize the importance of allowing your children time to understand, come to terms with the change, and learn how to cope with seeing you happy with someone else. It won't be easy, and it might take several attempts or meetings before your child expresses even a little eagerness about your new relationship, but know that with time, and with your ongoing support, things will get easier and feel more normal. Your priority is to protect and safeguard your child's feelings and wellbeing.

Telling Your Ex About Your New Relationship

The most frequent question I get asked about these days is whether there is a requirement or even a right time to tell your ex about your new partner. If you have been seeing somebody for a few months, is this a new relationship? Do you need to inform your ex?

Whether you ever need to tell your ex anything is a matter in and of itself. No one can force you to do anything and there is no rule that says you need to share any part of your new life. But having said this, my view will always be that you should do what is right and best for your children. At the end of the day, it is your children's future that you are obliged to protect and nourish. If your children know about a new partner and are forming a relationship with that person, there should be no pressure on your children to hide that new person from their other parent.

Children will always feel a little guilt or a need to protect their other parent's emotions, particularly if that other parent has not moved on and has not re-partnered. If you are purposely not telling your other parent, or requiring your children to keep your relationship a secret, you really are placing an unfair, emotional burden on your children.

If you can make your children's lives easier and less burden-some, my view is you do whatever you need to do to protect them from unease or pressure. This obviously will differ for children depending on age, maturity, and developmental stages. I can say that even for my preschooler, he showed some signs of stress and unease when telling me about what he had gotten up to over the weekend with his dad and his dad's new partner.

At first, he would be reluctant to include her name in conversation. But over time, and the more I encouraged free conversation about the topic and showed no judgment, the more comfortable he became. I could see his face light up when he could freely tell me about activities they had done together or her involvement in his day-to-day routine. Ultimately, what would be the point of me expressing any dislike or anger toward this person to my son? How would that benefit him? I much preferred being able to speak with him openly and see him happy and confident.

When I re-partnered and things became serious, I took the same approach. Once I felt it was something more serious, I decided it was time to share this with my son's dad—not because I was under any obligation to do so—but because I knew that was the fair thing to do for my son. This allowed him to go between homes telling stories and talking about the new people in his life without feeling any guilt, burden, or need to protect his parents.

Sure, we will still have the odd laugh when he comes back home and says to my partner and I things like, *"My daddy is stronger than you. He has bigger muscles and eats more steak."* That sort of comment pops up every few days, but we see it as a young child still wanting to protect the special relationship he has with his dad. That is not to say he doesn't adore my partner, but kids will be kids.

How much information you give your ex about your new partner will obviously depend on a variety of things: the type of relationship you have with your ex, the time you have been together with your new partner, whether there is a history of family violence to consider, and of course, how comfortable your new partner feels with the situation. It is no longer a matter of you only considering yourself and your ex and how that relationship might impact a situation, but now it is important you are cognizant of your new partner's feelings and wishes.

At first, you might just share the name of your partner, a few basic details, and reassure your ex that your new partner's role is not to replace them as a parent. Rather, your child now has the benefit of an additional person to love, nurture, and support them. They also have someone new to provide them adult guidance so they can benefit from experiences and learning opportunities. For me, providing that reassurance can make or break how your ex handles the situation. Of course, it's not your responsibility to protect your ex's feelings, but at the same, as I have said over and over in this book, anything you can do to make your child's life easier is a positive.

When, then, is the right time, if at all, for your ex and your new partner to meet? Perhaps the answer is never. That is fine if that is what is best for your situation. There may never be a time that feels for your new partner to meet your ex. When we start talking about blended families and even new children from new relationships, there is a likelihood that your new partner will become more involved in your children's lives. This might mean coming together for celebrations, school functions, or change-overs with your ex. Before that happens, I am big believer that there is benefit to having your ex meet your new partner, even if only for ten minutes. This will take away the awkward feeling of first meeting at a function, not only for you or your partner, but for your children.

I remember when my partner met my son's dad. The first thing my son said as walked through the shops afterward was, *"I'm so happy you said hi to my daddy. Now you are friends."* The look of satisfaction and calm on his face was priceless. As adults, we often let negative feelings override the true reality of a situation. At the end of the day, who cares who did what, who hurt who, or whether or not you like each other as people? The thing that matters is what your child takes away

> *"Stepparents are not around to replace a biological parent, rather augment a child's life experience."*
> —**Azriel Johnson**

from a situation. And if a five-minute meet and greet gives your child a stronger feeling of safety, security, comfort, or happiness, do it. Do it for your child. Put your child first and move forward to create a nurturing, albeit separated, family life for your child. It will mean everything to them.

Tools to Cope with Resistance to Change

The reality of any new relationship is that change is imminent. Your separation or divorce was already a significantly life altering event for your children, something that will impact them forever. Any change is difficult, whether it be positive or negative. As with all things, this requires us to adapt. It is, unfortunately, common for children to rebel against the idea of one of their parents re-partnering.

Many kids will even express an extreme dislike of this new person. This can cause problems for your new relationship but also for your existing relationship with your child. Seeing a parent date or be affectionate in a new relationship can be overwhelming and really confusing for kids. They are often challenged with the internal debate over why you weren't happy with their other parent or wonder what about their other parent made you so upset or angry. What is it about this new person that brings you joy?

It is likely confusing for a child to see you giddy and excited with a new partner, particularly if they have also experienced you at your lowest moments during a separation. Be mindful of this and respect the emotions your child is experiencing.

You might find that your children become suddenly possessive of you, particularly in the presence of a new partner. They will compete for your time and affection. This could be expressed in a way where they are observably rude to your new partner. They might ignore your partner or cut them off during conversations. They might grab your hand to take you away from your new partner during outings or at functions to assert their position and their possession of you. Children see things differently. Navigating these behaviors is fundamental to preserving your new relationship.

When you notice a negative change in your children after you have re-partnered, the best way forward is to maintain open and transparent communication. Be open to hearing what they have to say, even if it is hurtful or negative. This might include you asking:

- "Tell me what is troubling you and why you are upset?"
- "What questions can I answer about my relationship with (name)?"
- "How can I help you to feel more comfortable spending time with (name)?"
- "How often are you comfortable with seeing (name) at this point in time?"
- "What is making you uncomfortable when (name) spends time with us?"

- "Is there a way I can assist you to better understand this change?"

You won't be able to answer all your child's questions, and your conversations may not lead to any immediate positive changes, but by making time for your child to feel heard, you foster a secure environment for your child to be open, honest, and to feel heard.

I find that one way to encourage children to see the positive in a new relationship is by finding something that both your children and your new partner have in common. It might be a television show they both like or a sporting team. It might be that you both have children of a similar age or sex and this is something that is exciting and common. While teenagers can often learn to accept someone if they see this person making you feel happy, the younger children are, the harder it will be for them to accept a new partner simply because they make you happy. Younger children often need that sense of having something in common to encourage them to be more open and accepting.

It is easy to become defensive and stick up for your new partner when your child is being defiant about the new relationship. You might feel like this is the right thing and your child just needs to suck it up and be grateful. I have had so many clients who instinctively felt the need to discipline or challenge their child for their behavior toward a new partner.

My client, Giselle, had a hard time introducing her young teenagers to her new partner. They had been together for about ten months before she introduced him to her kids. They started by attending football games together. She would buy tickets to see her children's favorite team play and one time, invited her new partner. That turned into weekly dinners. As time went on, they all moved in together.

Giselle was over the moon at feeling like she had a real family back, but her teen boys hated the idea of their mom being in a new relationship. They spoke poorly toward her new partner, deleted messages from her phone when they came in, and acted out on purpose when he was around. This was something Giselle struggled with. She felt so scared to lose her partner that she prioritized his feelings over those of her boys.

Instead of speaking with them transparently to get to the bottom of what was going on in their minds, she would threaten them with having to live full time with their dad if they didn't get their acts together. She would tell them they were lucky to have a stepparent who supported her and bought them things. She would tell them there was no issue and that their concerns were not valid, their concerns were their problems and not hers.

She slowly started spending less time with her boys and more time with her new partner. Rather than improve the situation, she made things worse. It was only with the assistance of her family therapist that Giselle was made aware that what she really needed to do was prioritize her boys' feelings, spend one on one time with them without her partner around, and put boundaries in place to validate both her boys' feelings and her partner's.

This is not to say that she should have put up with, or even allow, her children to be rude or disrespectful to her new partner or to undermine him. It simply meant that she needed to look at what was going on at home and identify a way to improve the situation. Sometimes it is important for kids to have a time out from a partner, or to be disciplined away from a new partner. It is important to always be mindful that children often don't want their parents to separate and will always grieve the situation. Balancing the need for children to have one on one time with you, but also be involved with your new partner and get to know him or her, is challenging, but will get easier with time.

One of the best things a family can do when navigating these types of changes is to seek support and guidance from a qualified professional. A family therapist or counselor can offer support to you as a parent, your new partner, and your children, to ensure that children still feel loved and secure. It is often with the assistance of a good professional that relationships are improved and communication styles better developed to manage ongoing emotions and challenges at home.

Adjusting to a New Marriage with Children

Re-partnering after separation doesn't only mean you are navigating how this will impact your relationship with your ex or your co-parenting relationship. It doesn't even only involve how your children will cope with a new partner in your life. It can often also involve the blending of two sets of children and a whole new family dynamic.

How do you navigate being with someone who also had children of their own who have been through a separation or divorce? Things can seem messy. Perhaps your separation was amicable and your children have had the benefit of seeing their parents be friendly, social, and work together. Your partner's children, however, have been in the middle of a high conflict, toxic divorce and have come to know their parents as angry, bitter, and terrible toward one another.

A good friend of mine, Bernadette, re-partnered with a man who absolutely hated his ex. They would call each other the worst of names and could not even be on the same soccer field together when their daughter played. Bernadette and her ex were good friends. They chatted at changeover, still celebrated their daughter's birthday together, and generally were accepting of each other's new lives. This proved to be an absolutely challenge for Bernadette when she moved in with her new partner and both children started living together.

The children had been exposed to different separation styles. Now they had to navigate a new style of living as well as relationships with new stepparents. Bernadette's ex was happy for her and encouraged their daughter to be affectionate and respectful of Bernadette's new partner, whereas his ex-wife was a nightmare. She would send rude messages and turned their daughter off Bernadette. This made the home dynamic challenging. They needed urgent professional help.

When separated families blend, parents need to be cognizant that children probably have had different rules at home. Kids must get used to new partners and new dynamics. Teenagers in particular will struggle with being told what to do by a new partner or by being faced with a different way of doing things at home (more so if this is very different to how their other parent does things).

To assist in navigating a new home, parents need to ensure they are mindful and respectful of all children's points of view, open the forum for collaborative discussion about the household, and listen to each other, but also promote clear rules for what is expected. Sometimes what can best work is having discussions about each family's previous rules to help children understand what has worked in the past and what can work together as a new family.

Parenting as a team is so important when joining families. Try to always be on the same page as your new partner when it comes to how you approach your household. This means common rules on bedtimes, curfews, chores, and the like. Children should not be treated differently.

I'm often asked about how to promote a happier blended family home life, or how to encourage children to feel more comfortable with a new partner and children at home. I think there are a few tips to remember and to try and adapt within your new family:

Don't be overly affectionate with your own children in the presence of stepchildren. This can cause a divide and make children feel unwanted or neglected. Try to treat all children equally within the home. It is still okay to spend some one on one time with your biological children, but try to organize this around your stepchildren to avoid conflict and drama.

Don't push your stepchildren into being your friend or best friends with your children. Let nature take its course. Equally, don't push your child into being best friends with your new partner. Relationships will take time to grow and develop. The best thing you can do is to maintain a conflict-free environment, with common goals, mutual respect, and boundaries in place so that all family members feel respected.

Don't stop your children from communication with their other parent (your co-parent). It is important that children feel free to talk about and talk to their other parent in the presence of a stepparent or stepsiblings. Things for your child shouldn't change just because you have re-partnered.

> *"Blended families are a beautiful mix of diverse people who each serve an important role in our lives. At times, it can be challenging to appreciate everyone's unique beauty."*
>
> **—Deana Keller La Rosa**

Don't denigrate your co-parent or your new partner's ex, especially in the presence of any of the children. This will cause negativity and distrust within the home. No child wants to hear their parent, and especially not a stepparent, speak negatively about their other parent. This also applies to criticizing a co-parent's way of doing things or lifestyle. Just because you are happy and living in a new home doesn't mean your co-parent's way of life is any worse.

Be sure to keep up your co-parenting relationship, even when you are in a new relationship and have a new family. Prioritize time to speak with your co-parent about your children and their wellbeing and development. Notify your co-parent about significant changes or issues with might impact your children.

The Blurred Line Between Stepparent and Decision Maker

Setting boundaries when establishing the stepparent or blended family relationship is fundamental to ensuring consistency, security, and clarity for children. It can often be hard to manage emotions and expectations of both your child and your new partner when first cohabitating and blending your family.

How much help is too much? Can your new partner have a say in the way you raise your child? When does discipline cross the line? Does your ex get a say in the way your new partner disciplines within your home? Navigating these issues and working things out can feel overwhelming. As overwhelming as you find it, it is probably also difficult for your new partner to navigate where they fit in and understand their role within the home.

My friend Bernadette had a difficult time initially asserting any authority within her new blended home. Despite the fact that she was cooking, cleaning, doing school pick-ups and drop-offs, and essentially maintaining the home for her new partner and his children, she was unable to have any say over the discipline of his children.

His ten and twelve-year-old were very challenging. They would act out defiantly in her presence and would purposefully ignore her when she told them something was inappropriate and unsafe.

This then caused friction between Bernadette and her new partner's ex, who would send text message after text message accusing her of being cruel and unkind to the children. Was it Bernadette's partner's role to stand up and pull his children into line? Did Bernadette have to accept that it would take time for the new family to come together and for the children to accept and understand her role within the family?

I suggested that Bernadette needed to learn to respond and not react. Rather than becoming upset and causing conflict within the home, she needed to communicate more appropriately and together with her partner, establish appropriate ground rules and boundaries. My opinion is that it is totally fine (and even healthy) for a stepparent to create rules within a home and be firm about those rules, but it really is up to the biological parent to support their partner and affirm those rules.

The biological parent needs to make clear to their children that the rules should be followed and respected so that everyone can get along and the home can operate happily and peacefully. Every new relationship takes work, and when you throw children into the mix, particularly stepchildren, things can seem a thousand times more difficult. Couples often need to compromise on their style of parenting and find a balance between their differences. So, where does the role of stepparent impact the co-parenting relationship?

Your co-parenting relationship will naturally suffer turbulence when re-partnering. You formed a healthy communication style, established boundaries to protect your new relationship, and are getting on well for the sake of your child, but when a new partner comes along, they throw things into a little disarray. All of a sudden, you feel anxious about how your relationship with your co-parent will be perceived by your new partner.

How much communication is too much? Are there feelings of jealousy? Distrust? Your new partner suddenly wants a say in the way you discuss things with your ex and make decisions. My advice? First and foremost, make sure you and your new partner are a team. This person is the person you now share a life with and need to make important life decisions with. At the same time, you share an incredibly, wonderful thing with your co-parent—your child. This person still deserves your time, respect, and ability to communicate and make decisions about your child.

Rather than have your new partner inserting themselves into the co-parenting dynamic, be on the same page with your partner first. Work out where you both stand on an issue and what will work best for your child in your house. You can then take that to your co-parent and work with them to find a resolution. Three is often a crowd and it can make the co-parenting relationship destabilize, particularly if your ex has not re-partnered and might still be holding onto hurt or grief from your separation.

Your ex will have their guard up, so it's better to let them feel that it is only you two that are working together making decisions. If and when the time is right, there is no issue having discussions and making co-parenting decisions with your ex and your new partner collectively, but this needs to be navigated appropriately.

When we talk about what we can do within a blended family to help the transition feel smoother, my advice is that we do what we can to make our children feel secure and safe within their new home environment:

- Stepparents should avoid interfering or stepping into arguments between children and their biological parent. This can cause children to resent their stepparent and feel attacked.

- Be supportive of your partner in situations of conflict or boundary testing. Keep open communication and discuss what support you can provide each other.
- Work collectively to navigate change, conflict, and defiance amongst children.
- Avoid implementing totally different rules within your home to yours or your new partners' co-parent. Co-parenting is not a competition between homes. Where rules differ too much, discuss with your partner the best way of discussing this with a co-parent.
- Never (ever) denigrate yours or your partner's co-parent. Children want to feel that their stepparent is supportive of their other parent and is not there to be better than their other parent. You are not the new and improved parent.

Additionally, if a stepchild wants to vent about their other parent, don't contribute to negative discussion. Listen, allow the child to vent, but stay neutral. It's often more effective to be supportive but not encourage negative discussion. Your stepchild will make up with their other parent and you don't want to be the person who engaged in bad-mouthing them. This will only cause future conflict and distrust.

Finally, it is so important that parents do not pick favorites within a blended family. Gifts, celebrations, and discipline needs to be the same for every child within the family.

We know that two families coming together and blending into one will bring challenges and mixed feelings. There will be hurdles to cross and sometimes everything seems impossible.

A blending of families can also be the most beautiful, complete feeling for parents who have a second chance at happiness and stability for their future. Tread delicately. Be mindful of children's emotions and that things take time. Go slowly.

Recognize individual differences, fears, anxieties, and love will follow. Just as it took time for you to fall in love with your new partner, it will take time for each of your children to fall in love with your new blended family.

Eventually, things will fall into place and you will feel at home with your blended family. Define your family values and let your family relax into their new normal.

CHAPTER 8:

Tools Available Post-Separation to Avoid Court and Encourage the Co-Parenting Relationship

Resources to Avoid Judges, Conflict, and Upset

Collaboratively co-parenting does not necessarily mean you will be able to agree on every issue or have a co-parent who wants to work with you. Many separations or divorces do require intervention of a mediator or a lawyer to assist parties in jointly resolving their dispute. If there wasn't a need for family lawyers, I'd be out of a job!

One if the best parts of my job though, is the ability to work with a client who is high conflict, can't see past the hate and the anger, but over time, starts to see the benefit of open communication, joint decisions, and working collectively with their co-parent for their child's benefit. It is hugely rewarding when I experience two parents resolving their dispute together midway through the court process, removing the need for judicial determination.

I often also check in on my former clients, years after their matter has finalized, to see how they are progressing. You would be surprised how many high conflict couples who ended up at trial find a way forward once they have left lawyers. Litigious letters cease being sent, there are no longer threats of court rooms and judges, and they find a way to work together and co-parent amicably.

If you find yourself in a situation where you cannot come to agreement with your ex about your parenting arrangements, speak with your lawyer about options outside of the court system. There is still a way to do it collaboratively while also using a lawyer for support and guidance.

What Is Collaborative Practice?

Collaborative practice is a method of working toward settlement without litigation. Lawyers implement methods of dispute resolution, mediation, and negotiation through several collaborative meetings.

Parents will generally engage specially trained collaborative lawyers who work together over several of these meetings, often with mental health and (if a property settlement is also involved) financial experts, to negotiate a settlement.

The purpose of holding the meetings is to collaboratively work out details including parenting arrangements, division of assets, and other day-to-day issues which may affect a family. Parents work together to map out a pathway forward, then settlement documents are drafted, and the divorce is finalized.

Parents and their lawyers will enter into a participation agreement which contracts the team into finalizing the legal aspects of their separation without attending court. The goal is to then use interest-based negotiation to work toward a mutually beneficial outcome. The benefit of the collaborative meetings is that lawyers will balance needs and concerns with ideal outcomes. The role of the lawyers is to remain impartial and assist both parents in making decisions and resolving issues.

The collaborative coach will encourage and facilitate outcomes by focusing on needs and goals. The financial neutral will assist in gathering information from each of you and will summarize your financial position. They will often arrange business and real estate valuations and help you both understand your financial situation, current, and future cash flows.

A child expert or communication professional will often assist in developing a parenting plan, focusing on the needs and requirements of your particular family. They will also assist in navigating the difficult emotional aspects of your separation. The aim is to encourage a meaningful co-parenting relationship long-term.

The fundamental framework behind collaborative practice is to encourage open communication and transparency. The process really does encourage co-parents to work together by facilitating productive discussion and brainstorming ways to work toward resolution that suits each unique family. It is important to remember that no two families are the same and no two separation agreements will be the same.

Engaging in formal collaborative practice allows parents to come up with a plan for their family to co-parent and function as a separated family long-term, together.

One of the largest benefits of engaging in the formal collaborative process is that it can be the foundation for ongoing success in collaborative parenting relationships into the future. It is often the catapult that helps parents form a united approach to future decision making and responsibility.

The formal process encourages parents to put appropriate boundaries in place and learn to listen to and actually consider the other's needs, values, and parenting goals. A stronger co-parent bond is often formed with the help of lawyers, allowing co-parents to focus on their child's development and wellbeing as opposed to past conflict and hurt.

At the end of the day, a co-parenting relationship will always require an ongoing need for negotiation, compromise, and decision making. It can often be hard for newly separated parents to navigate this approach immediately following the breakdown of a relationship.

You can reach out to your local collaborative family law practice group for help in finding a collaboratively trained family lawyer near you. Local associations will also be able to assist you in finding other collaborative practitioners, including coaches.

Mediation Options

Another way of working with your co-parent to resolve your dispute is through the mediation process. Mediation allows you to work with a third-party mediator. This is a neutral person who assists you and your co-parent in making decisions about your children, and can often be done with or without lawyers. Mediation can take place together in the same room or via a process known as "shuttle mediation," where the mediator goes between rooms to facilitate discussion and negotiations.

The benefit of choosing to go through the mediation pathway with your co-parent is to encourage a forum for discussion about aspects such as custody or living arrangements, child support, and other issues regarding your children's future. When you engage lawyers, matters are often complicated and blurred by high conflict letters, threats for court applications, and time constraints that impact how deeply you can negotiate.

Mediation allows you the freedom to discuss all issues and come up with your own agreement about all aspects of your child's life. A good mediator will explore the ins and outs of a point of dispute and let you explore all options.

Mediators are usually trained lawyers or mental health professionals who have had significant experience in the family law sphere and understand the dynamics of child development and the impact of separation and divorce. They are often also skilled in understanding and recognizing the impact of family violence and trauma.

The mediator should meet with both you and your co-parent to understand the background to your dispute and encourage you to come up with a parenting plan that is in your child's best interests. The role of the mediator is to maintain impartiality in discussing different options and encourage you as parents to make your own decision. The purpose of mediation is not to call evidence or argue your case. Instead, it is to explore avenues for resolution and hopefully, reach agreement.

Unlike the court process, where a decision is made for you, mediation allows you and your co-parent to reach an agreement that best suits both of you, as well as your child. You have control over the decisions made and the plan to be in place for the future of your family. Just because you have separated does not mean important, life-long arrangements ought to be dictated to you by a court. You have the power to try to reach agreement with your co-parent and map out the best way forward.

To do this, you need to be in the mindset to compromise. Nobody wins in mediation. Both parties need to be child focused, reasonable, and willing to give in a little when it comes to coming up with plans and schedules. You may not "win," but you will know that you had the opportunity to have a say in your child's future, as opposed to leaving that to a judicial body.

Child Inclusive Mediation

In some jurisdictions, child inclusive mediation is available to assist parents to better understand how their children are feeling and what their views are in relation to ongoing family conflict and future arrangements. Generally, parents need to engage both a mediator and a child inclusive practitioner or a child consultant.

The child inclusive practitioner or child consultant will work with both the parents and the child to essentially be the voice of the child in the mediation process. They interview children and gather information about their personalities, schooling, mental health, development, and views so that this perspective can be echoed during the mediation process between parents.

It can be useful to parents to have a neutral third party be a representative for their child. This third party can bring the child's views to the mediation process to assist parents in considering their child's true perspective and focus on their desires moving forward. This also takes away the usual he said/she said debate between parents who each have a view about how their child feels.

Social science tells us that child inclusive mediation encourages higher rates of satisfaction amongst parents who have made decisions about their parenting disputes and that lower rates of parents turning to mediation use the court system. The ability to have a child's voice heard in the mediation process has proved a useful tool by encouraging partents to properly consider their children when making decisions.

Realistically, child inclusive mediation is appropriate for families with children who are at least of school age. Whether or not the process is suitable for a child will also come down to the dynamics of the family dispute, the mental health of the child, and their maturity/developmental stage.

Those who work as a child inclusive practitioner or child consultant are trained mental health professionals. They are skilled in discussing matters with your child in an appropriate manner that accounts for differences amongst children, their ability to process the separation, and understand what is happening.

Parenting Coordination

Parenting coordination has become increasingly popular, with parents moving toward engaging a parenting coordinator to assist in resolving issues relating to parenting arrangements. Parenting coordination assists separating and separated parents transition into co-parents through a non-confidential, child-focused alternative to the dispute resolution process.

The technique assists parents in the organization of ongoing parenting arrangements before, during, and after final Court Orders have been reached. The Parenting coordination process combines assessment, case management, dispute resolution, conflict and communication coaching, and sometimes decision-making functions.

It is particularly suited to parents who have had difficulty resolving child-related disputes, assisting former partners in becoming effective co-parents, and focusing on the needs of their children, rather than emotional disputes between themselves. A parenting coordinator is appointed to maintain focus on the best interests of children and assist in the development of constructive and effective communication skills between co-parents.

Parenting coordinators are highly experienced working with high conflict families and undergo specific parenting coordination training to develop the skills essential for their role. They will generally be a mediator, social scientist, or experienced family lawyer, and it is crucial for each individual family to consider the coordinator best suited to their personal circumstances and family dynamics. Parenting Coordination assists with:

- Dispute resolution arising out of the implementation of parenting orders
- Education about co-parenting and parental communication
- Focusing on the psychological and developmental needs of the children
- Strategies to manage conflict and reduce the negative effects on children
- Effective post-separation parenting

While parenting coordination may sound similar to counseling or therapy, it focuses on reducing a child's exposure to conflict by assisting parents' transition to a relationship of effective co-parenting, rather than one defined by conflict, anger, and hostility. Parenting coordination can be revisited at any time if parents feel they are returning to a conflict-based relationship.

Parenting coordination is also fundamentally non-confidential, unlike therapy, and is reportable in court. This means that both parties can be held accountable for their actions and behavior. Parties may be monitored to ensure compliance with relevant Court Orders and emails and messages may be monitored to evaluate communication skills for the identification of areas for improvement.

Family Therapy

Following separation and divorce, it is essential that parents recognize the need to support their children while also ensuring that the children maintain a meaningful relationship with both parents. This can be an emotionally complex task, which can become increasingly complicated by insufficient communication between parents.

Family therapy can assist parents and children with the emotional impact of separation, help parents communicate better, and allow greater understanding around the emotional issues and/or trauma a child may have.

Introducing family therapy relatively early following the breakdown of a parenting relationship will allow any underlying issues to be therapeutically addressed, and potentially resolved, without unnecessary court intervention.

In matters of high conflict, the court may direct a family to attend reportable family counseling to resolve issues that may have arisen and minimize harm to children. In reportable family therapy, a therapist will report the progress of the therapy to the court. The family practitioner may be called upon to provide an opinion regarding outcomes achieved in therapy and certain matters raised.

In other circumstances, a court may order that the parties and/or children participate in non-reportable therapy. This means that counseling is completely confidential, allowing the family to attend without fear that any information shared will be disclosed during their family law proceedings.

Advantages of non-reportable family therapy include parties feeling safe to discuss any issues in dispute, allowing families to confront and accept any damage which may have been inflicted, and assist in healing. The important relationship between the practitioner and the family is protected by the confidential nature of therapy, as practitioners are not required to disclose personal and private information to the court.

I am a big believer in the power of family therapy to assist with parenting issues, help rebuild relationships which have suffered as a result of the separation, and help parents adjust to their new roles as single parents. It is evident that therapy with a specialized family therapist can be a vital resource for families undergoing separation.

The reality of separation and divorce is that not all co-parents can work things out amicably. In many cases, lawyers will be engaged to assist in more cooperative engagement and to arrange visitation schedules and decisions for children. I am a seasoned Australian family law expert, and having navigated the co-parenting world myself, I know that co-parenting is tricky. Its fraught with conflict, lingering emotions, and it becomes emotional and complicated. When engaging a lawyer, I would suggest the following:

- Choose a family law specialist. The greater experience in divorce and family law, the better the advice you will receive.
- Don't automatically go for the "bull dog" lawyer. If your aim is to maintain an amicable relationship with your co-parent, choose a lawyer who respects your desire to work cooperatively with your co-parent and facilitates healthy, focused discussion, as opposed to encouraging high conflict court proceedings.
- Make sure your lawyer understands the background to your separation and divorce. Most lawyers will tell you the reason why you separated is irrelevant and try to minimize the hurt and the emotion you are experiencing. Knowing your background is important so they can best assist you

in both resolving your dispute and navigating a way forward that is palatable for you and your co-parent.

- Discuss options for mediation, collaborative practice, and family therapy with your lawyer. Lawyers should work holistically with other professionals who can assist you in resolving your divorce across all areas. This often means working with good mental health practitioners, financial advisors, forensic accountants, and parenting coordinators.
- Be open and transparent with your lawyer. It is so important to tell the truth and ensure your lawyer has all the facts.
- Don't get distracted by your co-parent's choice of lawyer. Even if they are weaponizing your child and playing the game, ignore them.

Above all, focus on what you want to achieve: nurturing your child's future and the ability for you and your co-parent to at least work toward a business-like relationship.

CONCLUSION

Co-parenting is a forever commitment. The relationship doesn't end when your child finishes high school or graduates university. You will have weddings, baptisms, holidays, and grandchildren to navigate. Your biggest responsibility as a co-parent will be raising your children and being a support to them throughout their life, despite no longer being in a relationship with their other parent.

Rather than focusing on the differences between you and your co-parent when it comes to parenting styles, communication, financial goals, and the negative history between you both, focus on facilitating a nurturing environment for your child's ongoing development.

Let your children be children. Let them enjoy their school years, play dates with friends, and trips to the park and museum. Let your children play their favorite music, dance in their bedrooms, and binge on popcorn and soda while watching a movie.

Don't let your children become caught up in the conflict between you and your ex. Don't let your children feel the pain and burden of your relational struggles and heartbreak. You don't want your child to be the one who dreads their parents both coming to watch the soccer game or water polo game because they know conflict will erupt. You don't want your child to be the one who hides school invitations to plays or concerts in fear of both their parents attending and causing a scene.

You do want your child to be the one who is excited for Christmases and birthdays because they know they will share it with two supportive parents, who, whilst separated, have shown unwavering support and commitment to the nurturing of their development. You want your child to be the one who is excited to Facetime dad while at mom's house to share achievements from school that day, without worrying what mom might think.

At the end of the day, taking a collaborative approach to your co-parenting relationship will bring about a safe, secure, and peaceful environment for your children. You will foster a future for your children where they feel that nothing has significantly changes in their lives, despite the separation, and that their parents still work together for their benefit.

Good co-parents work together to provide their children with a stable and reassuring life, which is crucial for a child's emotional and psychological wellbeing and imperative to a child's ability to adapt to new family dynamics as they grow.

Treat today as day one of your co-parenting journey. Be open minded. Be child focused. You have got this, and you will be a wonderful co-parent.

ABOUT THE AUTHOR

Gabriella Pomare has a passion for writing and family law. Her experience spans both media and law throughout a dynamic and rewarding career. The daughter of a family lawyer, she was always inspired to make a change in the world of separation and divorce.

She worked in journalism while studying law, writing for publications including *Cosmopolitan* and *Take 5*, before transitioning into law. Gabriella jumped into the role of Associate to a Justice of the Family Court of Australia before moving to private practice and joining her father, an established, accredited specialist family lawyer. Under Gabriella's vision, the firm grew from a sole practitioner practice to a modern, boutique firm with three offices.

Gabriella was a finalist in the 2018 *Lawyers Weekly 30 under 30 Awards* and nominated in the 2019 *Lawyers Weekly Australian Law Awards* as a "Rising Star of the Year." In 2022, 2023, and 2024, she was a finalist in the *Lawyers Weekly Partner of the Year Awards* for Family Law, and in 2023 and 2024 she earned her place as a finalist in the *Women in Law Awards, "Partner of the Year—SME."* She was also named in the 2024 top fifty women in the Australian legal profession by *Australasian Lawyer.*

Through her experience both working with separating families and navigating the co-parenting world herself, she gained a passion to help separating partners collaboratively co-parent. She firmly believes uncoupling does not have to break up the family unit. Today, Gabriella uses her expertise to help separated parents jointly grow resilient, secure children of divorce.

A free ebook edition is available with the purchase of this book.

To claim your free ebook edition:

1. Visit MorganJamesBOGO.com
2. Sign your name CLEARLY in the space
3. Complete the form and submit a photo of the entire copyright page
4. You or your friend can download the ebook to your preferred device

Morgan James BOGO™

A **FREE** ebook edition is available for you or a friend with the purchase of this print book.

CLEARLY SIGN YOUR NAME ABOVE

Instructions to claim your free ebook edition:
1. Visit MorganJamesBOGO.com
2. Sign your name CLEARLY in the space above
3. Complete the form and submit a photo of this entire page
4. You or your friend can download the ebook to your preferred device

Print & Digital Together Forever.

Snap a photo

Free ebook

Read anywhere